Collins

Aq
Fisn

Don Harper

First published in 2007 by Collins
an imprint of HarperCollins*Publishers*
77–85 Fulham Palace Road, London W6 8JB
www.collins.co.uk

Collins Gem® is a registered trademark of HarperCollins *Publishers*

08 10 11 09 07
2 4 6 5 3 1

Text by Don Harper; © HarperCollins *Publishers*
Photography, artworks and design © HarperCollins *Publishers*

Based on material from *Collins need to know? Aquarium Fish*

Created by: Toucan Books Ltd, London
Editor: Theresa Bebbington
Designer: Bradbury and Williams

All photographs taken by Neil Hepworth except:
Hippocampus-Bildarchiv: 117, 127, 149, 166, 167, 169, 176, 180
Interpet (01306 881 033): 18, 22, 23, 25
Artwork by JB Illustration

A catalogue record for this book is available from the British Library

ISBN-13 978-0-00-720579-0
ISBN-10 0-00-720579-1

Colour reproduction by Digital Imaging
Printed and bound by Amadeus S.p.A., Italy

CONTENTS

KEEPING FISH

There are few hobbies that are as relaxing, interesting and enjoyable as keeping an aquarium. Whichever fish you prefer, you can create different environments for them in a tank – where you can gain a unique insight into the natural world of fish.

THE APPEAL OF AN AQUARIUM

An aquarium does not require a large amount of space, and you can easily fit one in your home. There are also plenty of ways to arrange the decor in a tank to suit your tastes and the needs of the fish. With such a wide range of aquarium fish in an array of shapes and colours, there is certain to be at least one species that will appeal to you – in fact, you might find limiting the choice of fish for your tank is the most difficult part of keeping fish.

Breeding fish

As long as you care for your fish properly, there are a number of fish that you can breed and rear in the home aquarium, adding to the fascination of the hobby. Live-bearers such as guppies are the most straightforward to breed. However, successfully spawning some egg-laying species and rearing their fry can be a real challenge.

For the experienced fish-keeper, another possibility is the creation of new colour and fin variants in a fish such as those found in angelfish (*Pterophyllum* species) and swordtails (*Xiphophorus* species).

Links with fellow enthusiasts

There can be a social dimension to having an aquarium, with aquatic societies catering both for general fish-keepers and also specific groups of fish such as cichlids. Some of these organizations hold regular meetings, while others operate through the Internet, linking people around the world.

Mollies (*Poecilia velifera*) can become so tame that once they recognize you they will feed from your hand.

There are regular fish shows organized by aquatic societies, where fish are exhibited. Specific judging standards have been established for a number of the more common aquarium fish such as goldfish and guppies, which are bred in numerous fancy forms.

The benefits of fish-keeping

Scientific research into fish-keeping has confirmed that watching fish as they swim around in their tank is a relaxing activity. It can lead to a reduction in blood pressure, which brings direct health benefits. This helps to explain why aquaria are often found in stressful places such as dentists' waiting rooms.

Goldfish (*Carassius auratus*) are easy to keep.

An aquarium can provide a focal point of interest that can be shared by young and old alike, and a goldfish will make an ideal first pet for a child, as it will require minimal adult assistance. Fish-keeping is also an activity that can be enjoyed by those with disabilities, who may not be able to care for other pets that require more attention.

ACQUIRING FISH

If you live in a hard-water area, set up a tank for fish that naturally occur in this environment, such as cichlids from the Rift Valley lakes of Africa. If you have soft water, you can keep fish such as the discus (*Symphysodon* species) from the Amazonian region. Or modify the water chemistry in your tank (see pages 48–53) to keep a wider variety of fish.

White spot can be caused by stress (see page 162).

Fish size

Although most fish for sale are small because they are young, fish do vary in size. Some catfish and cichlids can grow 30cm (1ft) long and will become too big for your tank. Avoid overstocking the tank (see page 58).

Before choosing fish
You need to consider the following factors before you buy your fish:
• Water chemistry and temperature range
• Compatibility
• Adult size
• Ease of care and breeding
• Dietary needs (certain fish need special foods)

Getting along together

Many fish such as tetras live in shoals. They are docile, and you can keep them with nonaggressive fish that need similar water conditions, such as *Corydoras* catfish, creating a 'community aquarium'. Keep other fish with predatory natures on their own.

Aggressive behaviour occurs among the same species. Males of the Siamese fighting fish (*Betta splendens*) attack other species with similar colours, believing them to be rivals. Territorial disputes also arise at breeding time. Keeping odd numbers of fish such as a group of five creates greater harmony than pairs.

Good beginners' fish
- Goldfish
- Corydoras catfish
- Platy
- Dwarf gourami

Not for beginners
- Red-tailed black catfish (*Phractocephalus hemioliopterus*): grows large
- Honey gourami (*Colisa sota*): delicate
- Shark catfish (*Arius seemani*): predatory

Shopping for fish

Many pet stores stock common fish such as goldfish and guppies. For a wider selection visit an aquatic centre. Check the fish before buying them, inspecting all of the fish in the tank. Look for diseases (see pages 160–65). Minor inflammation on the fin occurs when fish have been recently moved. Once they are in a permanent home, it will heal. Healthy fish are brightly coloured, depending on the species, not pale, and should be well-muscled. Fish should swim easily, but some fish such as catfish are reluctant to swim.

Fish to avoid

A fish that floats at an abnormal angle is ill. If the body shape is shrunken towards the rear, it is an old or ill fish. Look for missing scales. Any damage to the body can lead to a fungal infection (see pages 162–64). Check the fins. Long fins ragged at their tips are okay, but be concerned if they are badly frayed, with signs of fungus.

Choose only healthy fish such as this African cichlid. Give them a final inspection while in a plastic bag to go home.

HOW FISH WORK

Fish rely on a pair of gills to extract oxygen from water. Water is drawn in through the mouth and flows over the gills, where oxygen enters the bloodstream and carbon dioxide diffuses into the water, which is then expelled from the body. If the fish is distressed or has difficulty in breathing, the gills move more rapidly.

Alternative breathing

Some fish that live in slow-flowing, stagnant and poorly oxygenated waters have an auxiliary means of breathing. They gulp air from the surface, which passes into their swim bladder. This organ allows the fish to adjust its position in the water. The anabantoids have evolved another method of supplementary breathing – special labyrinth organs near their gills.

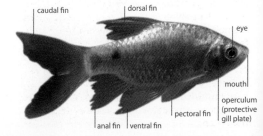

caudal fin | dorsal fin | eye

mouth

operculum (protective gill plate)

anal fin | ventral fin | pectoral fin

Bottom-dwellers

The appearance of most fish can provide clues about their lifestyle and the area of the tank in which they occupy. In bottom-feeding fish, such as loricariid catfish, the mouth is underneath the body. These fish are sluggish by nature, and their body shape allows them to lie on the base of the tank and hide.

Active fish

A fish with a streamlined appearance, often with a forked caudal fin that allows it to power through the water with minimum effort, will be an active fish. If it has upward-pointing jaws and a flat upper body profile – hatchetfish, for example – it lives and feeds close to the water surface. A fish that occupies the mid-water level such as a tetra has balanced jaws and a streamlined, symmetrical body shape.

External protection

Most fish have a covering of hard, overlapping scales to provide them with protection, but the size and shape of these scales vary. Some catfish, such as members of the *Corydoras* group, rely on bony plates instead of scales to protect their bodies. These restrict the fish's mobility. More active catfish in the *Synodontis* genus rely on well-lubricated, thickened skin as defence against predators and infections.

THE TANK

Setting up an aquarium is usually an easy procedure, and you can create a traditional or contemporary design without difficulty. You can choose from all-in-one units, incorporating everything you need, or buy the tank and the components separately. The most important decision to make is deciding where you want to position the tank before starting to equip it, because once it is full of water, it will be impossible to be moved without emptying it.

Tanks for kids

A coldwater tank is more suitable for a child caring for the fish on his or her own, as there is no risk of accidental burning when maintaining the tank. However, if a child wants to keep tropical fish, use a tank with an external tank heater and a separate thermostat. An acrylic tank will be safer and lighter for a child to handle than a glass unit, although its sides can be scratched.

SELECTING A TANK

The first main decision is whether you want to keep coldwater fish such as goldfish or tropical fish, which require a heated aquarium. The expense of running a heating system is low, and heaters that incorporate integral thermostats are inexpensive. In any case you will need a filtration system and a light over the tank, and these require an electrical supply.

Choosing a location

Decide where you want to place the tank before buying it, so that you can select one that will fit in the chosen space, considering both its size and shape. It is better to position the tank in the room where it will be against a wall out of direct sunlight, especially around the middle of the day, when the sun is at its

The rectangular tank is the most common type. It has a better surface area than round bowls or tower tanks.

hottest. However, brief morning sunlight can be beneficial on occasions, especially to encourage spawning behaviour in cyprinids and other species.

Aquarium designs

Glass tanks are made in a variety of shapes such as the traditional rectangular design, bowl shape and modern designs. You may not find an undergravel filter plate to fit over the entire base of an unusual-shaped tank, so you'll need another filtration method.

Triangular glass tanks are available to fit in the corner of a room. Most of these come with a cabinet and a hood. Remember that custom-made aquaria are expensive compared with more conventional designs.

Horizontal vs vertical
Avoid buying a tank in the shape of a vertical tower. It has little horizontal swimming space for fish and a small surface area compared with its volume of water. This creates a less efficient gaseous exchange, which takes place at the air-water interface, with carbon dioxide diffusing out of the water and being replaced by oxygen.

Stands

A free-standing tank without a cabinet can be supported on a stand, or it can be placed on a piece of furniture. Make sure that the furniture is sturdy enough for the weight of the aquarium when filled with water.

HEATING THE TANK

The aquarium heater usually fits inside the aquarium, where it must be fully submerged under water when switched on. Always allow it to cool before removing it from the tank. If you have a shallow aquarium – for killifish perhaps – use a short heater.

Heaters and watts

The output of heaters is measured in watts. The heat output your tank needs depends on the volume of the tank. Look for a table on the back of the package to help you choose the correct heater for your tank. As a guide, there should be 0.2–0.5 watts per litre (1–2 watts per imperial gallon). However, a tank with a large volume of water holds its temperature better than a small tank.

Internal heaters

Most internal tank heaters incorporate an integral thermostat, and this combined unit is

The size of the tank will affect the heater it needs.

known as a heaterstat. The thermostat controls the heat output from the unit and is preset to 24°C (75°F). You can raise the temperature slightly to encourage spawning by turning a knob. Otherwise, the preset temperature is suitable for a tropical aquarium.

The heaterstat fits at the back of the tank and there must be free circulation of water around the unit, so that colder water is brought into contact with the heater. Place it at an angle to allow the heated water to rise and be circulated by convection currents and pull cooler water into contact with the heater below. This creates a more consistent water temperature and prevents the heated water from contacting the thermostat and turning the unit off.

Heating choices

You need to consider the following points before heating an aquarium:
• Do you want coldwater or tropical fish (don't heat a tank for coldwater fish)
• Do you need internal or external heating (choose the latter for large and destructive fish)
• Do you want a traditional thermometer or an LCD thermometer

Undertank heat

An external heater in the form of a thin pad that lies under the base of the tank is the best choice for large fish or destructive fish that excavate the ground for food. You'll need a thermostat that fits within the tank to control the pad. Undertank heating is often preferred in a breeding tank. Use one if the water is shallow or if there is a risk of eggs being deposited on the heater.

Temperature readings

An aquarium thermometer ensures that the heating system is working. You can purchase the traditional internal thermometer, but external LCD designs with a colour strip are easier to read. Make sure you attach it properly to the outside of tank for an accurate reading. Place the thermometer at the farthest point from the heater, where the water is coldest.

For an oscar (*Astronotus ocellatus*) or other destructive or large fish, only use an external undertank heater.

LIGHTS AND LIGHTING

The lighting above a tank is not only essential for seeing the fish clearly – especially when looking for signs of a disease or indications that fish are ready to spawn – but it is also vital for healthy aquatic plants. The plants in the tank rely on light as a source of energy. It allows them to photosynthesize, where the plants use the carbon dioxide discharged by the fish and release oxygen into the water – which also contributes to the well-being of the fish.

Flourescent lights

Not all lights are suitable for an aquarium. Plants need to be exposed to specific wavelengths of light

The fluorescent tube fits in the tank's hood.

for photosynthesizing. You should use special fluorescent lights that mimic the effects of sunlight. They have the additional benefit of emitting light rather than heat, so they will not affect the water temperature – unlike ordinary tungsten bulbs. You'll need at least one full spectrum tube for photosynthesis.

Special lighting

You can run two tubes in parallel to include a tube to highlight the coloration of the fish along with a full spectrum tube. Or use a night light for fish that live in dark surroundings or for catfish and other species that become more active from dusk onwards.

The output of lighting varies, and more powerful lighting is necessary above deeper aquaria. There should be a minimum of 4 watts of light for each 4.5 litres (1 imperial gallon) of water.

Replacing the lights

The output from fluorescent lights declines over time, so it is recommended to replace them every nine months or so, even if they are still working. This will ensure that the plant growth remains healthy. When buying replacement fluorescent light tubes, make sure you take note of the size of your tank. The tubes are available in various lengths, and you'll need to purchase the correct size for your tank.

GRAVEL AND ROCKWORK

Gravel can provide an attractive base for your aquarium, but depending on your choice it either drains or enhances the colour of the fish. Rockwork can create an interesting focal point – and it gives fish that have a timid nature a convenient place to hide.

Choosing the gravel

The covering used on the base of the aquarium is important if an undergravel filtration system is fitted, because the gravel must be coarse enough to allow water to flow through its irregular shapes. There are various types of aquarium gravel available, some of

Natural dark gravel creates a neutral background for plants and won't distract from the colours of bright fish.

which are brightly coloured. However, these rarely work as well as natural stones because of the optical effect they create, and bright red gravel will drain the colour of red fish such as some swordtails (see pages 124–25) and goldfish (see pages 130–33). White gravel can result in the fish appearing paler than normal and cause them to react in the same way as if they were under bright lights.

Gravel comprising of natural stones will create a neutral background that shows off your fish. When assessing the quantity of gravel required, allow approximately 1kg (2.2lb) per 4.5 litres (1 imperial gallon), based on the tank's volume.

Rockwork

Rockwork helps to create a natural backdrop and provides retreats for the fish. It can also look attractive – but remember that its natural coloration appears brighter when it is wet. You can purchase various types of stone for an aquarium from an aquatic store, and these are usually sold on the basis of their weight.

Rockwork plan
It helps if you have a plan for your aquarium before purchasing the rocks to get an idea of where they will fit. Try not to cover too much of the base of the aquarium with rockwork, because this can affect the efficiency of an undergravel filter.

You can obtain artificial lightweight rockwork designed for use in aquaria. These are available at aquatic stores.

Choosing rockwork

Limestone rocks are unsuitable for tanks where soft, acidic water conditions are required. For fish that spawn on rockwork, include an inert rock such as slate in the tank. Position rockwork securely to prevent it from falling over. This can occur in tanks with active fish that dig in the substrate.

Cave fish

For fish that spawn in caves, a better option is to use a clean section of a clay flowerpot. Place it on the floor of the tank rather than trying to create a cave from loose rocks that can collapse.

FILTERS AND WHAT THEY DO

Filters are needed to maintain a healthy environment in the tank. There is a choice of undergravel filters, power filters and external filters. They break down the fishes' waste and assist oxygenation of the water.

Fish in a tank live in higher densities than in the wild. There is no flow of water to flush out their waste, which accumulates in the tank and threatens their health. Filtration helps to remove the ammonia made by the fish, so it is essential in maintaining a healthy environment. It also saves the need to empty the tank on a regular basis, which is distressing for the fish.

Waste breakdown

The ammonia from the fish and the decomposition of other waste matter such as any uneaten food is detoxified by a series of chemical reactions

An undergravel filter fits over the base of the tank.

that occur due to beneficial bacteria that live in the aquarium. This detoxification forms part of the nitrogen cycle, in which the ammonia is broken down to nitrite and then to nitrate, which in turn can be used by plants in the tank as a fertilizer. This is the result of biological filtration.

Is the filter working?

To monitor if the filtration system is effective, make sure you carry out water tests, using a kit available from an aquatic centre, to check the water's pH (see page 50) on a regular basis. These will alert you to problems that can endanger the fish.

New tanks

In a new aquarium you will need to seed a biological filter with a culture of bacteria, which can then multiply in the aquarium. You can add zeolite to remove ammonia before the biological system is fully effective, which may take up to two months.

Undergravel filtration

An undergravel filter is a simple type of biological filter. There must be a good water flow through the gravel above it so that there is enough oxygen for the bacteria to thrive. A coarse gravel is needed for this purpose at a depth of 5cm (2in) above the filter plate. An air pump is also necessary. It should have a non-return valve to eliminate the risk of water running

Beneficial bacteria populate the foam core, which has several layers of foam. The foam core also traps waste.

back into the pump, and it must never be covered, as this presents a fire risk.

Power and external filters

Many tanks have a power filter consisting of an integral pump and a foam core. It relies on both biological and mechanical filtration. Position it with the outflow just at the surface to increase oxygenation in the water by creating a current.

Bigger tanks can use an external filter hidden in a cabinet. It draws water out of the tank and passes it through a filtration system, which may include activated carbon. This carries out chemical filtration, binding chemicals extracted from the water. External filters are not suitable for fish treated with medication.

There is a range of more complex filters and other media on the market. Trickle filters draw water from the tank and oxygenate it as it runs through the filter.

PLANTS

Aquatic plants will provide a natural backdrop for the fish in your aquarium, and they also fulfil a number of important roles. They offer vital hiding places, especially at breeding time, and utilize the waste produced by the fish, creating a better environment. Live plants can also provide a source of food for some fish, and they are sometimes used for spawning. However, live plants may not thrive under all conditions, so sometimes lifelike plastic aquarium plants may be preferable.

Some fish such as the zebra danio (*Brachydanio rerio*) enjoy nibbling on Canadian pondweed (*Elodea canadensis*).

Fish with a timid nature such as the tetras feel more at ease in a tank with plenty of plants where they can hide.

PLANTS AND SNAILS

Both living aquatic plants and plastic plants have their place in the tank, adding to its appearance and creating retreats. Ornamental snails are sometimes kept in a tank, but they are often considered invasive.

Plastic plants

Realistic-looking plastic plants do not detract from the overall appearance of the aquarium, and they are easy to incorporate in the design of the tank. Plastic plants are often supplied with a weighted base, which you can simply bury under the substrate, or you can weigh it down by other tank decor if the fish like to excavate the substrate.

Living plants

Growing living plants in the tank requires time, but they create a more natural environment and improve water conditions for the fish. Choose the plants carefully to ensure they will not outgrow the tank. Keep them in small pots to ensure that their roots do not spread too far through the substrate. If allowed to spread, the roots can block the holes in an undergravel filter, reducing its efficiency.

You can use plastic and living plants together.

Caring for plants

The way in which living aquatic plants are treated will have an impact on the ease in which they can be established in new surroundings. Always handle them carefully and never allow their leaves to dry out. When you purchase new plants, submerge them in water of the correct temperature at soon as you can.

It is not uncommon for some dieback of the leaves to occur after moving a plant into a new position, particularly in more delicate species. However, as long as the environmental conditions are suitable, new growth should soon appear. The lighting in the aquarium (see pages 18–19) is important at this stage, and it may help to use a special aquatic plant fertilizer until the plant becomes established.

A variety of plants creates the best habitat for fish.

Snails

Aquatic snails are easily introduced to a tank by accident as eggs on the leaves of new plants. The egg masses are transparent and jelly-like in appearance. While a few snails add a focus of interest in the tank and their scavenging feeding habits may help to clear up uneaten food, they often breed so readily that their numbers can become overwhelming. The vast

Some snails such as the golden apple snail (*Pomacea bridgesi*) need warmer water conditions than others.

number of snails will soon destroy the aquatic plants on which they feed. It is hard to curtail the breeding habits of snails because they are 'hermaphrodite' – they have both male and female sex organs in their bodies. Keeping only two snails together results in the production of fertile eggs.

Avoiding snails

The best way to control aquatic snails is to remove egg deposits from the tank before they hatch. There are some aquarium fish such as the green pufferfish (see page 153) that will prey upon snails, and they may even eliminate them from a tank.

CREATING A PLANTING SCHEME

To work effectively the plants in a tank should merge with other decor such as rockwork and bogwood. It is also important to consider the habits of the fish, using the plants to complement their behaviour.

Providing retreats

In a community aquarium with a variety of fish, you'll need plants in different parts of the aquarium. If you include surface-dwellers among your fish, then provide floating plants, which they can hide below. Within the main body of water, place plants in several areas, which again can be used as hiding places, but at the same time make sure you leave an open area where the fish will have plenty of room to swim.

Visual appeal

The needs of the fish are important, but also consider the appearance of the plants in the tank.

You can use a planting stick to position a plant.

Some plants can be uprooted by fish with scavenging habits such as catfish. Keep these plants weighed down.

Establish the height to which the plants will grow. If you want to emphasize the width of the aquarium, position smaller plants in the foreground and around the sides of the tank, and allow them to merge with larger plants towards the back. This arrangement will also make it easier for you to watch the fish. You can add a single, more striking specimen plant in the central area, towards the back of the tank.

Some degree of trial-and-error will be necessary as you blend the plants alongside other aquarium decor. You should start with a selection of plants that will not outgrow the size of your tank. Be careful not to plant the aquarium too heavily at first and allow for the growth of the plants.

Bogwood

An important planting medium in the tank, pieces of bogwood are available from aquatic stores. This type of wood has been submerged in a boggy area for a long period, and during that time it becomes full of tannin, which will turn the aquarium water yellowish. Before adding bogwood to your tank you should soak it in water, changing the water regularly until it stays clear.

Bogwood retreat

You can attach plants such as Java moss (*Vesicularia dubyana*) to the bogwood with an elastic band until it anchors itself. The bogwood will provide cover under which bottom-dwellers can

Plants and bogwood are a retreat for bottom-dwellers.

hide. Once established, its thick growth will provide retreats for the young fry of live-bearers such as guppies (see pages 120–21). Java fern (*Microsorium pteropus*) also grows well on bogwood.

A DIRECTORY OF AQUATIC PLANTS

Aquatic plants can be divided into two categories: those that are anchored in the substrate and those that float on the water surface. Substrate plants can be subdivided into tall background and space-fillers, low-level plants and specimen plants.

Choosing plants

When choosing plants for the tank, it is important to not only consider their size, but also other factors that

Use specimen plants such as this swordplant (*Echinodorus* species) to make an attractive highlight in the tank.

influence their growth such as the water and lighting conditions in the aquarium. Before purchasing aquatic plants you should examine their condition. Healthy plants will be well-coloured, appearing green rather than yellow.

Sprigs, roots, bulbs

Aquatic plants may be sold as sprigs, which will root easily in the substrate, or as rooted plants, sometimes displaying offsets. You can purchase some plants in a dormant form such as bulbs, which simply need to be potted up.

Let Canadian pondweed (*Elodea canadensis*) float or weigh it in the substrate.

Aquatic plants do not usually require a soil-based growing medium, but if you pot them up, you'll need to use a special aquatic soil for this purpose. It is available in aquatic stores specializing in ponds, as well as some garden centres.

Floating plants

Plants that float along the surface of the water will have long roots that dangle in the water, and they are wafted around by the surface currents. These plants are usually fast growers and require regular pruning. They make excellent retreats for young fry as well as surface-dwellers. Make sure you include them in a breeding tank that is being used by bubble-nest builders.

Substrate plants

Aquatic plants that grow in or close to the base of the aquarium are known as substrate plants. They vary significantly in size, and also in terms of the growing conditions that they normally require. Although these plants are decorative, they are

The straplike leaves of vallisneria may be curled.

also functional, providing fish a place to hide from aggressive fish or for laying eggs.

Plants for different fish

Although these plants are suitable for many fish, they are especially beneficial in certain situations:

• **Vallisneria**

An ideal plant for angelfish (*Pterophyllum* species, see pages 102–3), as its tall, reedlike shape enables the tall, narrow-bodied fish to weave between the fronds. The straplike leaves may be straight or twisted.

• **Fairy moss** (*Azolla caroliniana*)

Suits bubble-nest builders such as Siamese fighting fish (*Betta splendens*, see pages 70–71). It is the ideal plant for providing anchor points for their nests.

• **Tropical hornwort** (*Ceratophyllum submersum*)

Useful as a spawning plant because it catches and retains the eggs as they drift downwards.

• **Amazon swordplants** (*Echinodorus* species)

A good choice for a tank housing fish that may destroy aquatic vegetation such as the oscar (*Astronotus ocellatus*, see pages 100–1) – these tough plants grow quickly.

• **Java moss** (*Vesicularia dubyana*)

It can create an attractive covering on rockwork and bogwood, making a retreat for bottom-dwellers such as the clown peckoltia (*Peckoltia vittata*, see page 80) as well as provide an ideal retreat for young fry of live-bearers.

• **Mangrove species**

Will thrive in a brackish water tank, which is preferred by the molly (*Poecilia velifera*, see pages 126–27).

FLOATING PLANTS

Duckweed (*Lemna* species) is a small plant that grows readily over the surface of the aquarium. Add

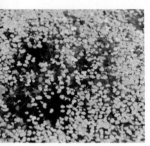

a few pieces to the tank and it should multiply rapidly. It thrives in brightly lit conditions. Although it is often found in coldwater tanks, you can grow it in a tropical setup too. Duckweed provides food for some vegetarian fish.

Duckweed can form a dense mat in your tank.

Fairy moss (*Azolla caroliniana*) is another plant adaptable to many water temperatures – however, it prefers relatively hard water conditions. The plant requires bright illumination to encourage its growth. Young fry will often cluster between its dark roots. Fairy moss is an ideal choice in an aquarium where diffused lighting is needed.

Water lettuce (*Pistia stratiotes*), or Nile cabbage, is so-called because of its appearance, as it looks like a floating vegetable. It requires a heated aquarium with a sufficient gap between the water surface and the hood to allow ventilation, which prevents the plants from damping off and rotting. Like most other floating plants, it will be wafted around by surface currents.

Indian fern (*Ceratopteris thalictroides*) is an unusual plant as it will grow well if planted in the substrate – however, it can also grow just as easily as a floating plant at the water's surface. In fact, old plants will produce buds that float up to the surface, where they develop. It is an ideal choice for an Amazonian tank with soft and acidic water conditions.

Crystalwort (*Riccia fluitans*) does not grow on the surface of the water but is usually found just below it, forming dense clumps. It provides good protection for young live-bearers, helping them to remain out of reach of the adults. It grows rapidly, by vegetative division, so just break off pieces from an existing plant to create new growth.

Floating fern (*Salvinia auriculata*) grows in long chains of oval leaves, which shade parts of the tank to help prevent algae. With proper light and nutrition it grows quickly, so thin it on a regular basis to ensure substrate plants receive enough light. To propagate it, simply break a piece off the main plant.

SUBSTRATE PLANTS

Sagittarias, a diverse group, thrive in heated water. They spread by runners, forming dense stands of growth. Some species grow taller than others. The dwarf sagittaria reaches 15cm (6in) in height, making it ideal for the sides of the tank.

Vallisnerias, or tape grass, have straplike leaves. They are valued for their adaptable growing habits, but they tend to grow better in a heated aquarium.

Canadian pondweed (*Elodea canadensis*) is popular in coldwater tanks. It is a good choice in a tank with goldfish, which often dig in the substrate. If pieces start to become leggy, cut off and retain the top 7.5cm (3in) – the shoots will grow rapidly.

False tenellus (*Lilaeopsis brasiliensis*) grows to only 7.5cm (3in) high, so it is ideal for the front of a tank. The strands create a grasslike area. It adapts to lighting, but does not thrive at high temperatures.

Variegated hygrophilia (*Hygrophilia* species) has reddish and purple hues that complement both green plants and the colour of the fish. The plant is ideal for a tropical tank and thrives in a range of water conditions.

Cryptocorynes are a versatile group, with up to 30 varieties available for tropical aquaria. They are adaptable in their water chemistry needs, and some thrive in brackish water conditions. Cryptocorynes are often sold as cuttings. Some need more brightly lit surroundings than others. Check on the growth of individual species – some can become tall.

When combining substrate plants, consider their leaf shape and colour, as well as the plant's height.

TANK SETUP AND CARE

Setting up a tank is usually a simple procedure, but check that everything is functioning properly before purchasing the fish. Otherwise, if something does go wrong such as the heater failing, the fish will be stranded in their transport bags until you can resolve the problem. Maintenance is also easy, but it can be more time-consuming until the filtration system is fully operational.

PREPARING A TANK

Start by rinsing out your aquarium in case the interior is dusty or there are spicules of glass from the manufacturing process. Then put the tank in position on its base, which must be level to lessen the water pressure on the joints at the corners of the tank. Check the levelness by using a spirit level. If the floor of the room slopes,

All tank equipment must work before adding fish.

adjust the position of the furniture or stand by using wooden blocks to ensure the tank is level.

If you have an all-glass tank, place it on a sheet of polystyrene to absorb any minor unevenness in the surface of the base. If you use an undertank heater, sandwich it between the polystyrene and the tank so that it directly contacts the underside of the tank.

Adding a backdrop

If you want to use a backdrop, carefully secure it in place. This will conceal anything behind the tank such as a patterned wallpaper, which may otherwise spoil the natural appearance of the tank. It is usually better to choose a neutral backdrop that extends the aquarium theme, rather than one that has a non-aquatic design, which could distract from it. Backdrops are available in various designs and sizes to fit aquaria of different sizes.

The filter

If using an undergravel filter, put the filter plate inside the tank directly onto the base. Make sure the uplift tube is fitted along with the airline, which will be connected to the air pump.

The gravel

Before placing the gravel in the tank – even if it is pre-washed – rinse it in a colander until the water runs clear. If you don't rinse it, the water will become cloudy in the tank. Once the gravel is clean, tip it gently into the tank, then create a slight slope running

from the back of the tank to the front. This will help you to find uneaten food that may rot out of sight.

The tank decor

Put in any tank decor such as rockwork or pieces of a clay flowerpot, but first scrub it with a clean brush to remove any dirt. Position the rockwork firmly in the

aquarium, burying it slightly into the gravel to prevent any dirt from accumulating around it. Make sure you allow sufficient space to put plants in at a later stage, as well as bogwood. You can add various

decorative items such as airstones, which create
bubbles to help circulate the water.

The heaterstat and power filter

Put the heaterstat in place, but do not connect it to
the power supply. The same applies if you are using a
power filter with the undergravel filter or on its own.
Position the power filter by one of the side panels,
with the output nozzle directed along the length of
the tank to create a good current. Avoid positioning it
with a rock or similar obstruction in front, which may
affect the inlet to the filter. Place the thermometer
inside the aquarium or on the glass at the front –
keep it away from the heaterstat.

Filling the tank

Reserve a clean watering can for adding water to the
tank. Place a clean container or a saucer on the gravel
and pour the water onto it to minimize disturbance
to the base. You should
use water from the
coldwater supply –
treated with a water
conditioner to neutralize
chlorine or chloramine –
rather than mixing it
with hot tap water. This
will ensure that the

heaterstat is working effectively – switch it on once you have filled the tank with water and allow it to heat the water. You can monitor its effectiveness with the thermometer. (Never switch the heaterstat on out of the water – this is dangerous.) Do not forget to add a beneficial bacterial culture. It will help to seed the filter bed and is essential before you can add the fish to the tank.

Adding the plants

Once the water temperature has stabilized, after about a day, set the plants in place, following your planting scheme. Position them by hand, or use a planting tool if the plants are not in pots to avoid

disturbing the surrounding area. For floating plants, allow them to drift over the surface.

The finished tank

Connect the lights and make sure that they are working properly. Over the next day or two, monitor the water temperature to make sure the heaterstat is also working. If it is, then your aquarium is ready for some fish (see pages 54–59).

Cover glass

The hood will take a pair of fluorescent lighting tubes

Place the thermometer where it will be easy to read but away from the heaterstat

WATER

Aquarium fish can be found in a range of different water conditions around the world. All water has the same chemical formula of H_2O, but it can differ in its relative hardness and acidity, which is measured on the pH scale.

Hard water and soft water

When rain falls the water is free of mineral salts. However, the chemical constitution of rainwater changes when it comes into contact with the ground, especially in a limestone area. This mineral is soluble in water, and by running over and through limestone rocks, calcium salts dissolve in the rainwater, creating 'hard water'.

Acidic water

If you need to produce more acidic surroundings in a tank, you can add aquarium peat – it may come in a sachet or you might need to add it to the filter. In the case of tetras, you can use a blackwater extract to add tannin, which wll help to acidify the water.

If you live in a hard-water area, the tap water will not form a lather when you wash your hands with soap, due to the presence of calcium salts. Fresh rainwater or water that has not run through limestone is described as 'soft', and it creates a lather rapidly.

Altering water composition

You can separate some calcium salts such as calcium bicarbonate from hard water by boiling the water. This is what happens when kettles fur up because of calcium deposits. This is known as temporary hardness and is abbreviated 'KH' (from the German *karbonate*). You can measure the relative hardness of water, using a test kit available from aquatic stores.

You can alter the chemical composition of tap water due to a process known as reverse osmosis (or 'RO'). This entails using a membrane to extract the dissolved chemicals to create softer water. To make the water harder, add limestone to the tank.

To raise the pH in an aquarium, you should add limestone rockwork or gravel.

pH and its significance

In water chemistry the pH reflects its hydrogen ion concentration. This is linked to the hardness of the water – hard water is alkaline while soft water is acidic. The water pH is measured on a log-based scale running from pH 0.0, the most acidic side of the scale, up to pH 14.0, which is the most alkaline reading; pH 7.0 is neutral.

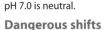

Dangerous shifts

A shift of only one unit is a tenfold increase in the hydrogen ion concentration in the water. A change of one unit can have serious consequences for fish.

In the aquarium environment, the breakdown of waste as part of the nitrogen cycle can impact the pH. It falls as the level of dissolved pollutants increases. The pH shifts are more dangerous in tanks of alkaline water.

Goldfish prefer relatively soft, acidic water.

SPECIAL WATER CONDITIONS

Most commercially bred aquarium fish can adapt to changes in water conditions, but some fish are more sensitive to water chemistry than others. The amount of salt in the water can make a difference to some fish.

Commercially bred fish

Most freshwater aquarium fish are bred on special farms around the world, in centres ranging from Florida to Singapore. These farms are often far away from their natural habitat, so the fish have adapted and are far less sensitive to water chemistry than their wild relatives.

Mollies, like this chocolate sailfin, thrive in slightly brackish water.

Nevertheless, there are exceptions. Certain fish such as many of the barbs live well in hard-water conditions – however, they are more likely to spawn successfully in soft, acidic water, like their wild relatives. If the water conditions in the tank are not optimal, the fish will probably lose some of their coloration and appear duller than usual.

Many gobies come from marine water, but the bumblebee goby (*Hypogymnogobius xanthozana*) likes brackish water.

Water salinity and brackish aquaria

The salinity of the water can be important, especially for fish that prefer brackish water conditions. Creating suitable water conditions for these fish is easy due to the availability of specially formulated marine salt. Follow the package instructions carefully because they differ slightly between brands.

The amount of salt required to create brackish water in a tropcial tank is less than is necessary for a marine tank. To add the salt, measure it out and dissolve it in the appropriate volume of water, stirring it with a wooden spoon. It may be necessary to make it in batches. The actual volume of water required is the total volume of the tank, which is easily assessed by multiplying the length, width and height together in centimetres and dividing by 1000, to give a figure in litres. Subtract ten per cent as a guide from this total to allow for the tank decor and equipment, which will give you the functional volume of the tank.

Maintaining brackish water

Once the tank is established, avoid switching between salt brands when carrying out partial water changes. If the water level falls because of evaporation, top up the tank with only fresh water, treated as always with a dechlorinator. It is the water that has evaporated, not the salt. If you add a fresh salt solution, you will increase the overall salinity within the tank.

Fish originating from estuaries, such as the green pufferfish (*Tetraodon fluviatilis*), often require brackish water.

ADDING FISH TO THE TANK

You can encourage newly purchased aquarium fish to settle into their new home by helping them adjust gradually to the water conditions and surroundings in your aquarium. The first few days will be the most important ones because extra stress can make the fish more vulnerable to disease.

Before you shop for fish

Before purchasing your fish, make sure everything is working correctly in your aquarium setup. You should wait for a minimum of a day or two to make sure the heaterstat is functioning properly. You may not want to buy all the fish for the tank at the outset, because the filtration system will not be working at maximum efficiency.

Buying the fish

Fish are usually supplied in plastic bags that have a small volume of water compared with the enclosed oxygen. However, there will be enough water to allow the fish to be transported safely home.

Inspect the fish in the bag before purchasing them.

Before adding new arrivals, float the plastic bag in the tank until the water temperatures are the same.

Do not delay your journey and travel with the fish carefully. Never leave them in the back of a car, for example, in direct sunlight. Keep the bag upright, and ensure that it cannot roll around to minimize the stress on the fish. You can wrap the plastic bag inside newspaper to create a dark environment for them or to provide insulation in cold weather.

Preparing to release the fish

When you arrive home, float the plastic bag at the surface of the aquarium for 20 minutes. This allows the temperature of the water in the bag to warm up gradually, so that when you release the fish, the temperatures in the bag and tank will be similar, placing less stress on the fish. You may not need to do this for coldwater fish because the temperature difference may be less significant.

Releasing the fish

The safest method for adding the fish to the tank is to use a net. Nets of various sizes are available for aquarium fish. The easiest way to transfer a fish is to pour the water carefully out of the bag through the net into a bucket. Place one hand over the top of the net while the fish is inside it, so that the fish cannot jump out as you move it into the tank. Lower the net, then turn it to one side and wait for the fish to swim out.

Settling in

Don't be surprised if the fish are shy at first and hide among the plants or rockwork. Leave the tank lights off for a few hours to allow the fish to become familiar with

Water in transport bags
Avoid tipping water from a plastic transport bag straight into the tank with the fish because there can be harmful microbes such as fungal spores present. Although these may not normally cause disease, they can multiply in a new aquarium, representing a potential hazard. It is better to net the fish to transfer them to the tank.

their new surroundings. After a few hours offer them a little food – they won't eat much.

Check the fish for the first few days to ensure they settle in and remain healthy. Avoid overfeeding the fish, as uneaten food will pollute the water and endanger their health. At feeding time, observe the fish at closer quarters and see if they are eating well.

How many fish?

Add about 50 per cent of your total stocking density at first, then wait another six weeks before adding more fish. This will allow the bacteria developing in

By using a net to release the fish into your aquarium, you will avoid the possibility of adding contaminated water.

the filtration system, which feed on fish waste, to become fully established. However, if you add other fish later, they may be harried by the established tank occupants. You can introduce new arrivals at feeding time when the other fish will be distracted, or with the lights off. You will risk introducing illness to the established fish, unless you quarantine the new fish for two weeks in another tank. If you add all the fish at once, you'll need to monitor the water chemistry closely and do more partial water changes.

Stocking capacity

To determine stocking capacity for your tank, allow about 1.5–2 litres of water per 1 cm of fish (1 imperial gallon per 1 in). It is important not to stock the tank to its maximum capacity when first setting up a tank because the fish need space to grow. You can use the figures in Fish Profiles (see pages 67–153) to determine a fish's adult size. The formula is only a general guide.

Clean water

Invest in a gravel cleaner to keep the substrate clean and do partial water changes. These are important in a new aqaurium setup, as they prevent the build-up of dangerous nitrogenous waste in the water, which can threaten the health of the fish.

The influx of fresh water dilutes the waste in the tank, making it safer for the fish, and helps to lessen the

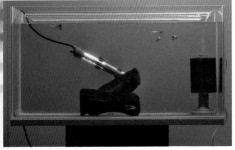

If you notice signs of illness in any of the fish, place them in a quarantine tank to safeguard the other fish.

burden on the filtration system while it is not functioning at maximum efficiency. Adding the compound zeolite also helps, because it binds ammonia. Daily water tests in a new aquarium is the best way of determining the state of the water.

Doing a partial water change

Change one-third of the water each week until the filtration system is working efficiently. Before adding new water to the tank mix it in a bucket with a water conditioner to neutralize the chlorine or chloramine. Add hot tap water to adjust the water temperature, using a thermometer to make sure the temperature is the same as the water in the tank.

ONGOING MAINTENANCE

Even when the aquarium is well-established, it will still need partial water changes, although less frequently. You'll also need to clean the gravel and foam filters and to prune the plants. By performing these tasks regularly, you'll keep your fish healthy.

Routine partial water changes

For a well-established aquarium, carry out partial water changes about once every three weeks, depending on the water test results. Use a gravel cleaner, which has a plastic attachment on a siphon tube for drawing water out of the tank.

Gravel and mulm

Cleaning the gravel is important because a brownish accumulation of fish waste, known as mulm, can be drawn down between the stones, making an undergravel filter work less effectively. You can clean the gravel easily with a gravel cleaner at the same time that you carry out a partial water change.

Using a cleaner

Start by placing a bucket on the floor, below the level of the aquarium. Fill the tube of the gravel cleaner with dechlorinated water, and place your thumb over the bottom end to prevent the water from running into the bucket.

Lower the gravel cleaner attachment over the gravel before releasing your thumb from the lower end. Water will flow freely out of the tank, with the gravel being stirred up.

Move the cleaner over the gravel, taking care not to uproot any plants and avoiding curious fish. When the bucket is almost full, place your finger over the end of the tube and lift it up to break the flow.

The gravel cleaner will only lift up the gravel partially.

Replacing the sponge

You may need to replace the sponge, but a new sponge will be devoid of bacteria, reducing the effective level of filtration in the aquarium. Reseed the filter with a bacterial culture. This applies in the case of similar media used in canister filters too.

Until bacteria are established, the water may have a build-up of nitrogenous waste. Some fish are more tolerant than others, notably those that originate in slow-flowing stretches of water or ponds, compared with those found in turbulent waters, where the flow prevents the build-up of chemicals. The major danger period is after about a week, when the ammonia level is at its peak. The nitrate levels will then rise and the filtration system will be mature after about a month.

Avoiding an overload

Do not overload the filtration system during this crucial period. You can do so by overfeeding the fish, with the wasted food decomposing in the tank. A surge in ammonia can also be triggered by the unnoticed death of a fish. For this reason, overstocking the tank can be dangerous.

Cleaning a foam filter
If you have a power filter, do not discard the old tank water from cleaning the gravel. Dismantle the filter to remove its foam and squeeze it out in the bucket of old tank water to remove the mulm. Do not clean it under a tap, because the chlorine or chloramine present can kill the bacteria in the foam.

Aquarium lighting

It can be difficult to establish the correct level of lighting in a new tank. If it is too low the plants will not thrive, but if the lights are left on for too long algae will thrive. If the growth of these microscopic plants

When you replace a sponge, keep a close watch on fish that prefer fast-moving water such as swordtails.

begins to develop into a problem, try reducing the length of time that the lights are on.

Algae overgrowth

The risk of algal overgrowth is especially high in a tank without live plants because the algae has no competition for the nitrate in the water. Some algal growth is natural and will be beneficial in the tank, providing a fresh source of food for certain fish, but you need to keep it in check. If algal growth starts to develop on the aquarium glass, remove it using either a magnetic or long-handled cleaner.

Take particular care when using a plant fertilizer of any type in a new aquarium. It is more likely to be the algae that will benefit rather than the plants.

Aquarium plants

You will need to spend some time attending to the needs of the plants. Plants turning yellow and dying back is common in a new tank, but the plants will eventually become established in their surroundings. Once they do, you may need to divide up clumps of some plants if they begin to take over. You can replant the younger growth, which is more vigorous. If you add any newly purchased plants, make sure you rinse them off carefully to remove any snail eggs. This is often how snails are introduced to a tank.

Trim off old shoots on a plant that start to turn yellow and die back – this pruning encourages healthy new growth.

FISH-KEEPING ROUTINE

Daily

• Check that the fish are eating well. Look for any fish that are off-colour or that have died unexpectedly – remove these without delay.

• Ensure that all the electrical equipment is functioning correctly. If not, try to find the cause, which may lay outside the aquarium. An air-pump hose might have become kinked after being moved, or a plug might have been inadvertently turned off.

Weekly

• Check the levels of ammonia and related nitrogenous chemicals at about the same time. Write the figures down, so you can monitor how the filtration system is working.

At feeding time, observe all the fish to make sure they are eating normally.

• Monitor the pH in a similar fashion.

• Remove any leaves that are obviously dying back, before they begin to decay in the tank.

Monthly

• Do a partial water change at least once a month in an established aquarium. Replace the removed water with dechlorinated water of the same temperature, tipping it into the aquarium carefully to avoid disturbing the decor and the fish.

• Look for any signs of imminent breeding behaviour in the fish such as females swelling in size or males becoming more territorial. Transfer breeding fish to a separate breeding tank if necessary.

Use a net to move breeding fish to a breeding tank. For bigger fish, be careful that they don't leap out of the net.

FISH PROFILES

A wide selection of the most popular aquarium fish are covered in this section. The entries are divided into the main family groupings. Before choosing fish for your aquarium, you should always check the requirements of individual species carefully – a difference in water-chemistry needs, for example, may preclude otherwise compatible species from being kept together.

ANABANTOIDS

This group of fish is represented in both Africa and Asia, but it is the Asian species that are the most widely kept and bred.

SURFACE-BREATHERS

These fish often live in shallow, stagnant water in the wild. This water has a low oxygen content, so they have a special labyrinth organ located above the gills on each side of the head. These enable them to come up to the surface to breathe, and the air from the labyrinth organs is absorbed into the bloodstream. If shallow water evaporates, some species can drag themselves over land to pools of water.

The males often build a nest using bubbles of mucus. Some bettas are mouth-brooders, with the eggs collected and retained in the mouth of the male until the fry hatch. Bubble-nesting fish produce thousands of eggs at a spawning; mouth-brooders, 10 to 50 eggs.

Do not use a power filter in the tank when bubble-nest builders are breeding.

PARADISE FISH

Macropodus opercularis

These anabantoids can live in unheated water at room temperature or in a typical heated tank if the water conditions are adjusted gradually.

Keep the aggressive male fish apart. A male fish may also bully an intended mate, so add a number of retreats in the tank, dividing the space with rockwork and plants to provide cover.

KEY FACTS

Family Belontiidae
Size 12cm (4¾in)
Water Soft and acidic
Distribution Korea, China and Japan
Habitat Rice paddies, slow-flowing water
Compatibility Males are aggressive
Diet Prepared foods and small live foods

This male paradise fish has longer fins than a female.

SIAMESE FIGHTING FISH

Betta splendens

These stunning fish range from vivid shades of red through blues and violets to black. There is also a whitish variant, known as the Piaket or Cambodian betta, and a yellowish form too. Fin variants include the crown, which has trailing tips to its fins; the split-tailed, which has a divided caudal fin; and the round-tailed. Siamese fighting fish are short-lived, with a life expectancy of about two years. Because it is impossible to determine the age of adult fish, choose juveniles if they are available.

Housing Siamese fighting fish

As their name suggests, male Siamese fighting fish are aggressive by nature. Never keep males together

because the weaker male will be killed, and even the survivor may be seriously injured.

You can house a single male without problems in a community tank. However, it is important to ensure that there are no similarly coloured fish that might be mistaken

The female is easy to identify by her small rounded caudal fin.

The male Siamese fighting fish has long, flowing fins.

for another betta in the tank – it may be attacked. For example, if you have a red Siamese fighting fish, do not house it with a red-tailed black shark (see page 134).

It is equally important not to include certain species such as tiger barbs (see page 141) in the same tank, because they will probably nip at the Siamese fighting fish's flowing fins.

KEY FACTS

Family Belontiidae

Size 5cm (2in)

Water Soft and acidic

Distribution Thailand and neighbouring countries of south-east Asia

Habitat Ditches, ponds, rice paddies

Compatibility Males are highly aggressive

Diet Prepared foods and small live foods

PEARL GOURAMI

Trichogaster leeri

The long fins on this species make it a target for fin-nipping fish.

KEY FACTS

Family Belontiidae
Size 15cm (6in), but often smaller
Water Soft, acidic
Distribution South-east Asia, from Thailand to Java and Borneo
Habitat Rainforest streams
Compatibility Peaceful
Diet Prepared foods and live foods

When choosing companions for pearl gourami being kept in a community tank, make sure they don't tend to nibble on long fins. Pearl gourami are peaceful, although males may be quarrelsome when in breeding condition.

You can tell the sex of a pearl gourami once it grows to 7.5cm (3in). A male develops a reddish coloration on its underparts, which is more intense when it is in breeding condition. The dorsal fin on the back and the anal fin along the underside of the male's body also develop elongated tips, but these are less conspicuous if the water quality is poor.

SPOTTED GOURAMI

Trichogaster trichopterus

The popularity of the spotted gourami has led to a number of colour variants, including a golden form, and a marbled variety. Spotted gourami are easy to keep but males do not get along, so keep them apart from each other and males of related species. You can mix pairs with other, non-aggressive fish.

KEY FACTS

Family Anabantidae

Size 15cm (6in)

Water Soft and acidic

Distribution Much of south-east Asia

Habitat Slow-flowing water

Compatibility Males are aggressive

Diet Prepared foods and small live foods

There may be either two or three spots on the fish's body.

MOONLIGHT GOURAMI   *Trichogaster microlepis*

Sleek in appearance, thanks to its tiny scales, the moonlight gourami is a silvery colour, aside from the reddish marking on the top half of its iris. The long pelvic fins, located just below the gills in these fish, enable them to be sexed. They have a reddish hue in males, but are yellower in females. In contrast, the pectoral fins, which are much more conventionally shaped, are located just behind the gills.

Under no circumstances should these or other related species be accommodated with barbs or other fish that may attack their long, trailing pelvic fins. Tetras will make suitable companions.

Moonlight gouramis are shy by nature and require cover within the tank.

KEY FACTS
Family Anabantidae
Size 15cm (6in)
Water Soft and acidic
Distribution South-eastern Asian mainland
Habitat Slow-flowing water
Compatibility Choose companions carefully
Diet Prepared foods and small live foods

DWARF GOURAMI

Colisa lalia

These beautiful, small gouramis are brightly marked, especially in the case of the orange and blue male fish. The female fish has a more silvery appearance. Breeders have also created a range of colour varieties, including the popular blue and the red or 'sunset' form.

The males have orange and blue banding on the sides of the body.

You can keep dwarf gouramis with other nonaggressive fish that have similar water requirements. Even the males of this species will get along reasonably well together, provided that the tank is not overcrowded and it incorporates various retreats, which can be constructed using rockwork and plants.

KEY FACTS

Family Belontiidae

Size 6cm (2½in)

Water Soft, acidic

Distribution Parts of north-eastern India and Bangladesh

Habitat River-drainage systems

Compatibility Peaceful

Diet Prepared foods and live foods

KISSING GOURAMI

Helostoma temminckii

The silvery-pink form of the kissing gourami is commonly available today.

KEY FACTS

Family Helostomatidae

Size 30cm (12in)

Water Soft and acidic

Distribution Thailand, Malaysia, Sumatra and Borneo

Habitat Large areas of water such as lakes

Compatibility Not usually aggressive

Diet Prepared foods and plant matter

These anabantoids are so-called because of the way they link their lips together, as if they are kissing. However, this is not a display of affection – it represents a trial of strength, with the weaker fish letting go after a contest that can last for 20 minutes.

Most kissing gouramis available in aquarium shops are silvery-pink, but a mottled variety has also been bred. Mature females may appear broader from behind.

Kissing gouramis are vegetarian. This means that they may damage any plants growing in their tank, as well as feed on algae and sometimes dig in the substrate.

CATFISH

There are over 2,000 species of catfish, including the loricariids, which may be identified by the 'L-numbering system', assigning each variety a unique number.

THE VARIABLE CATFISH

While some catfish are sedentary, vegetarian bottom-dwellers, others are active predators. These hunters seek other fish after dark, when they are easier to catch. Catfish have sensory projections called barbels around their mouth, which help them to swim safely after dark and find food. The size of the barbels can indicate the behaviour of a species – those with long, narrow barbels are more active and predatory. Catfish lack scales, but some have body armour.

Many catfish dig in the substrate in search of food.

BRONZE CORYDORAS

Corydoras aeneus

Corydoras catfish do well in a community tank, staying at the bottom of the tank, while other fish swim above them. Every so often, they swim to the surface and gulp some air to supplement the oxygen extracted from the water through their gills. Feed these fish special catfish pellets, thawed bloodworm and similar live foods.

KEY FACTS
Family Callichthyidae
Size 7.5cm (3in)
Water Soft, acidic
Distribution From Trinidad across northern South America to Argentina
Habitat Rivers
Compatibility Peaceful
Diet Prepared foods and live foods

The depth of the coloration of bronze corydoras can differ.

GREEN CATFISH

Brochis splendens

This small catfish looks like a *Corydoras* species, but its dorsal fin is longer with more rays. Their requirements are similar, although the green catfish often prefers deeper water.

This fish has a distinctive emerald-green body.

Create a naturalistic setting by incorporating a number of retreats on the floor of a tank. Bogwood is ideal for this purpose. You can keep green catfish in small groups, and they get along well in a community tank.

Sexing is difficult when the age of the fish is unknown. As a guide, pick the biggest and smallest fish available, assuming they appear healthy. Females grow much larger than males, and their underparts may sometimes have more of a pinkish hue.

KEY FACTS
Family Callichthyidae
Size 7.5cm (3in)
Water Soft, acidic
Distribution Upper Amazon, in Peru, Ecuador and Brazil
Habitat Rivers
Compatibility Peaceful
Diet Prepared foods and live foods

CLOWN PECKOLTIA

Peckoltia vittata

The inoffensive nature of clown peckoltia makes it ideal for a community tank of Amazonian fish. Make sure that a tank for these nocturnal catfish is well-planted, and create a number of retreats. Bogwood is important because these fish rasp their mouthparts on the wood. They appear to need this in their diet.

KEY FACTS
Family Loricariidae
Size 10cm (4in)
Water Soft and acidic
Distribution Amazon region of Brazil
Habitat Rivers
Compatibility Peaceful
Diet Prepared foods and greenstuff

Feed clown peckoltias at dusk, when they become active. They will keep algal growth in control, and it should be present in the tank before adding the fish. The algae make it easier for the fish to acclimatize.

The clown peckoltia does not dig or disrupt plants.

SPOTTED PLECO

Hypostomus punctatus

These inoffensive but large catfish are known as suckermouths, due to the suction-like mouth on the underside of the body. The mouthparts allow the fish to anchor itself to rockwork or wood to help prevent the fish from being swept away

The patterning of the suckermouth varies between individuals.

by a strong current. They also use bogwood for rasping their mouthparts. These fish can be destructive towards the vegetation in a tank, uprooting plants. Choose hardy, fast-growing plants and set them in pots.

Suckermouths eat tablets, and they like fresh foods that they can rasp. Among their favourite foods are sliced cucumbers and courgettes.

KEY FACTS
Family Loricariidae
Size 30cm (12in)
Water Soft and acidic
Distribution Southern parts of Brazil
Habitat Rivers
Compatibility Can be territorial
Diet Prepared foods and greenstuff

TEMMINCK'S BRISTLENOSE CATFISH

Ancistrus temminckii

These small loricariid catfish are ideal occupants for a community aquarium, although they can be territorial towards each other. Adult pairs can be recognized easily because the male fish develops bristles on its head.

Aside from browsing on algae growing in the aquarium, these catfish feed on a wide range of greenstuff, including fresh peas, red lettuce and even spinach. In a new tank, provide these foods in larger amounts to compensate for the lack of algae. These catfish will also eat small live foods.

The shy Temminck's bristlenose catfish are active after dusk.

KEY FACTS
Family Loricariidae
Size 12.5cm (5in)
Water Soft and acidic
Distribution Much of northern South America
Habitat Rivers
Compatibility Can be territorial
Diet Prepared foods and greenstuff

ANGEL CATFISH

Synodontis angelicus

The angel catfish is also known as the polka-dot catfish.

Synodontis catfish are known as the naked catfish because, instead of armour, they have a thick skin covered with mucus to protect them from injury. The even-spotted pattern is most prominent in younger fish, who are less grey than adults. The adults swim upside down to eat algae. These fish are more active at dusk, when they like to feed.

KEY FACTS
Family Mochokidae
Size 18cm (7¼in)
Water Relatively soft and acidic
Distribution Cameroon and Zaire
Habitat Slow-flowing, even stagnant water
Compatibility Not aggressive
Diet Prepared foods, greenstuff and small live foods

BANJO CATFISH

Dysichthys coracoideus

The banjo catfish is a bottom-dweller, living near the substrate. They like a sandy base, where they can dig, with pieces of bogwood, which will provide cover. The adult catfish may sometimes prey on aquarium snails, although they will also readily take pellets and hunt out worms. You can keep banjo catfish in small groups.

KEY FACTS
Family Aspredinidae
Size 12.5cm (5in)
Water Relatively soft and acidic
Distribution Amazon basin
Habitat Slow-flowing, even stagnant water
Compatibility Not aggressive
Diet Prepared foods and live foods

The body of this catfish resembles the musical instrument.

GLASS CATFISH

Kryptopterus bicirrhis

Because these catfish have no dorsal fin, they propel themselves by using their elongated anal fin, which extends along the underside of the body, and their caudal fin. Their long slender barbels not only help them find food but may also enable them to communicate with each other. It is not unusual for an entire shoal to rest in the water with their heads all pointing in the same direction.

Keep these naturally active catfish in a group of six, with plenty of space for swimming in the tank. Glass catfish are easy to keep, but they are susceptible to white spot (see page 162).

The transparent body highlights this fish's skeletal structure.

KEY FACTS
Family Siluridae
Size 15cm (6in)
Water Soft and acidic
Distribution Eastern India across south-east Asia
Habitat Fast-flowing water
Compatibility Highly social and not aggressive
Diet Prepared foods and small live foods

CHARACIFORMS

This group includes the tetras, the distinctive hatchetfish and some species that grow to a much larger size, such as the striped anostomus – and the notorious piranhas.

The tetra, a characiform, often has a coloured area on its eyes.

TETRAS AND THEIR RELATIVES

The characteristics of characiforms as a group are not clear cut, but most have a small adipose fin along the top of the lower back, between their dorsal and caudal fins. Virtually all species have teeth that may be as far back as the pharynx in the throat, but their feeding habits are diverse. They range from fearsome carnivores such as the piranhas to the *Metynnis* species, which are herbivorous by nature.

Many characiforms display strong shoaling instincts, especially those that tend to be popular in fish-keeping circles such as the tetras. All are egg-layers, and you can often recognize the male fish by their brighter coloration or more elaborate fin shape.

NEON TETRA

Paracheirodon innesi

Characiforms

You can often identify the sex of a neon tetra by the bluish stripe on its body. On a female the stripe is slightly broader, closer to the tail and not as straight as in a male. Only purchase brightly coloured neon tetras; they are susceptible to the untreatable neon tetra disease, which will result in loss of coloration. Keep neon tetras, which prefer the middle area of the tank, with other nonaggressive species.

KEY FACTS

Family Characidae
Size 4cm (1½in)
Water Soft, acidic
Distribution Eastern Peru, South America
Habitat Shaded waters
Compatibility Peaceful, shoaling
Diet Prepared foods and live foods

Neon tetras look best in a shoal of at least five fish.

BLIND CAVE FISH *Astyanax mexicanus*

Blind cave fish are adept at finding food in an aquarium.

Living in the darkness of caves has led to the loss of colour and eyesight in the blind cave fish. The fry hatch with normal eyes, but skin grows over them, making the fish dependent on the sensory input from their lateral line to find food, avoid danger and mate.

You can keep them in a community tank. Diffuse the lighting by adding floating plants.

KEY FACTS

Family Characidae

Size 10cm (4in)

Water Medium-hard and alkaline

Distribution San Luis Potosí region of Mexico

Habitat Underground rivers

Compatibility Can be a fin-nipper – separate from long-tailed fish.

Diet Prepared foods and live foods

BLACK NEON TETRA

Hyphessobrycon herbertaxelrodi

The beauty of the lively black neon tetra is apparent when in subdued lighting and good water conditions. They do best in small shoals, but you can also mix them with groups of other tetras. Distinguishing between the sexes is not easy, but the body profile of the female is more rounded.

KEY FACTS
Family Characidae
Size 5cm (2in)
Water Soft and acidic
Distribution Taquari River, Mato Grosso, Brazil
Habitat Tributary of the Paraguay River
Compatibility Social
Diet Prepared foods and live foods

Black neon tetras have a golden-green stripe.

LEMON TETRA

Hyphessobrycon pulchripinnis

Like many tetras, these fish have a bright red area above the pupils of the eyes. Do not confuse lemon tetras with the yellow tetra (*H. bifasciatus*), which lacks this reddish marking, and also the yellow and black streaks at the front of their anal and dorsal fins.

Keep lemon tetras in a well-planted aquarium that mimics their natural habitat, with some open areas where the fish can shoal and swim freely as a group. These tetras prefer the middle region of the aquarium, so they are compatible with hatchetfish (see page 96), for example, which remain close to the surface, and small catfish such as corydoras (see page 78), which swim beneath them.

The silvery-yellow colour can be seen on the lower surface of the body.

KEY FACTS

Family Characidae
Size 5cm (2in)
Water Soft and acidic
Distribution Ranges quite widely through the Amazon basin
Habitat Mainly found in streams
Compatibility Social
Diet Prepared foods and live foods

CARDINAL TETRA

Paracheirodon axelrodi

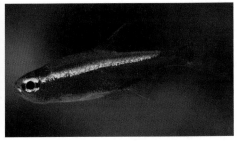

This tetra has a red stripe along the underside of its body.

Peaceful by nature, brightly coloured cardinal tetras are easy to keep. Their only special requirement is diffused lighting over their tank, which you can achieve by including floating plants at the surface. Keep cardinal tetras in shoals because this is how they live in the wild.

KEY FACTS
Family Characidae
Size 5cm (2in)
Water Soft, acidic
Distribution North-western South America
Habitat Shaded waters
Compatibility Peaceful, shoaling
Diet Prepared foods and live foods

BLACK WIDOW TETRA

Gymnocorymbus ternetzi

You can determine the age of these tetras by their patterning, which is less distinctive on young fish. The colour of the anal fin is blackish at first, turning greyish by about a year old. Sexing is simple because the anal fin is longer at the front in males and females have a more rounded body shape.

Black widow tetras make an ideal introduction to the group. There is also a long-finned strain of these fish, which are popular among fish-keepers. A shoal of naturally active black widows is not suitable for an aquarium accommodating more nervous companions – these are boisterous fish, although not aggressive.

KEY FACTS
Family Characidae
Size 5cm (2in)
Water Soft and acidic
Distribution Parts of southern Brazil, Bolivia and Paraguay
Habitat Rivers with tall vegetation
Compatibility Social
Diet Prepared foods and live foods

Black widow tetras have three black vertical bars running down each side.

GLOWLIGHT TETRA

Hemigrammus erythrozonus

Glowlight tetras will thrive in a small group.

KEY FACTS
Family Characidae
Size 5cm (2in)
Water Soft and acidic
Distribution Essequibo basin of Guyana
Habitat Rivers with aquatic vegetation
Compatibility Social
Diet Prepared foods and live foods

The reddish-golden stripe of the glowlight tetra has a luminous quality. This fish also has a reddish mark at the front of the dorsal fin. It is active by nature. It prefers visiting open areas rather than hiding among the vegetation. Females have deeper bodies and are a slightly larger size.

RUMMY-NOSE TETRA *Hemigrammus bleheri*

There is often confusion between this species and the red-nosed tetra (*H. rhodostomus*), which is also called the rummy-nose tetra. *H. bleheri* has more red on the head, extending to the body. Both tetras need similar care and are sensitive to water quality. Make water changes regularly. Don't overfeed – uneaten food pollutes the water.

KEY FACTS

Family Characidae
Size 5cm (2in)
Water Soft and acidic
Distribution Rio Vaupés in Colombia and the Río Negro, Brazil
Habitat Rivers with aquatic vegetation
Compatibility Social
Diet Prepared foods and live foods

H. bleheri does not have any black on the anal fin.

X-RAY FISH

Pristella maxillaris

If you keep X-ray tetras in a brightly lit tank, the subtle coloration of these fish will be obscured. The red of their caudal fin and the yellow area on the dorsal fin will appear washed out.

It is best to keep X-ray tetras in groups. Keep them in a community tank with other types of nonaggressive fish. Or create a 'themed tank', with plants and other fish that can be found alongside X-ray tetras in the Amazon region such as the glowlight tetra (see page 93) and marbled hatchetfish (page 96). Along with subdued illumination, a dark substrate in the tank will show off the fish's subtle coloration.

The internal organ known as the swim bladder is more rounded in females.

KEY FACTS
Family Characidae
Size 5cm (2in)
Water Relatively soft and acidic
Distribution Venezuela, Guyana and Brazil
Habitat Slow-flowing waters in the Amazon region
Compatibility Social, associating in shoals
Diet Prepared foods and some live foods

MARBLED HATCHETFISH *Carnegiella strigata*

The pattern on each marbled hatchetfish is different.

KEY FACTS

Family Gasteropelicadae

Size 5cm (2in)

Water Soft and acidic

Distribution Northern South America

Habitat Rivers with floating vegetation

Compatibility Social

Diet Prepared foods and surface insects

The curved underside of the hatchetfish is similar to the sharp edge of an axe. The top line of the hatchetfish is flat and its mouth is upturned, features indicating a fish that lives near to and feeds at the surface.

These fish will leap out of the water to catch a passing insect or glide some distance to avoid a predator, so keep their tank covered at all times. By including floating plants at the surface, you will provide hatchetfish with a greater sense of security. Hatchetfish like a diet that includes insects such as fruit flies or tiny crickets. They are vulnerable to white spot (see page 162).

CICHLIDS

One of the most popular groups of all aquarium fish is the cichlids. However, this is an aggressive group, so cichlids tend to be housed in pairs or groups on their own, and many species are not suitable for a community aquarium.

THE AGGRESSIVE CICHLIDS

Cichlids can grow large, and they may be predatory in their feeding habits. Keeping a number of cichlids in an aquarium can be disruptive, where they dig up the substrate and plants. As they grow older, separate a group into individual pairs to prevent fighting.

Some cichlids lay eggs in the open or in caves, watching over them and the fry once they hatch. In other cases parental care has progressed, with the female fish collecting and carrying her eggs in her mouth for two weeks or so, until they hatch. Only then will she start to feed again, but she still allows her offspring to dart back into her mouth if there is danger.

Many males are aggressive, and some may injure females when spawning.

DISCUS

Symphysodon discus

These cichlids are so-called because of their circular body shape, resembling that of a discus, but up until six months of age, they have an elongated profile.

Today's discus are far removed from their wild ancestor. The commercially bred fish are more brightly coloured than their wild relatives, although these fish do display distinctive regional variations, and green, brown and bluish strains can be identified from specific localities across their wide range.

A second, more localized species, called Heckel's discus (*S. discus*), has also contributed to the strains being bred today. You can see its influence in the broad, dark-coloured 'Heckel band' that runs vertically down the centre of the fish's body. Eventually, you should be able to recognize a particular fish by its individual head patterning.

The striking coloration is an appealing feature of the discus.

Soft-water fish

Discus have special requirements when it comes to keeping them in a tank. They need soft-water conditions and because of their height, they also require a deep tank. In addition, they will benefit from adding a blackwater extract.

Pairing up fish

If you purchase these fish when about 10cm (4in) long, it will be possible to sex them because the female's profile is more rounded. For breeding purposes, it is usually better to start with young discus, rather than introducing two or more adults together – the adults are less likely to be compatible.

Alternatively, you can keep a group of discus in a large tank together, and allow them to form pairs among themselves. The pairs will swim together, remaining in close contact at all times.

The male discus develops a hump on the forehead as he matures.

KEY FACTS
Family Cichlidae
Size 20cm (8in)
Water Soft and acidic
Distribution
Throughout the Amazon region
Habitat River systems
Compatibility
Peaceful and social
Diet Special discus food and some live foods

OSCAR
Astronotus ocellatus

The oscar grows to a large size and needs a spacious tank. An oscar can become friendly, even recognizing its owner and taking food from his hand. If you want an oscar to behave in this manner, start with a young fish, which can be tamed more easily than an adult. It is normal for oscars to excavate the substrate in search of edible items.

Colour variations

Oscars are less colourful when young, with a different pattern of markings. These consist of dark and light areas of marbling, but without the obvious reddish-orange areas seen on an adult.

KEY FACTS
Family Cichlidae
Size 35cm (14in)
Water Soft and acidic
Distribution Parts of the Paraguay, Orinoco and Amazon rivers
Habitat Rivers
Compatibility Best housed individually or in pairs
Diet Prepared foods and bigger live foods

Young oscars lack the orange-bordered dark spot near the tail.

The albino oscar still has reddish areas on its body.

The patterning of oscars differs widely, with some fish displaying more extensive orange coloration than others as they grow older. This is probably a reflection of the differences in wild populations. Captive-breeding has focused on developing strains that have bright orange-red coloration, which can be emphasized by feeding the fish colour foods. There are also striped and albino oscars. Domestication of the oscar has also resulted in the creation of long-finned oscars, but these have not become especially popular.

The red tiger strain has distinctive reddish stripes over its body.

ANGELFISH

Pterophyllum scalare

These distinctive cichlids, with their tall, flattened body shape, are occasionally recommended for a community tank when young. Unfortunately, they often do not thrive in these surroundings, because their long, trailing fins are attacked by other fish in the tank. Conversely, their rate of growth is often much faster than that of the other tank occupants, and when larger the angelfish may retaliate by persecuting their companions instead.

The gold-headed angelfish has a golden colour restricted to the head.

If you want to keep these elegant fish, set up an aquarium specifically for a small shoal of them. Select a tank that is relatively deep to take account of the fish's unusual shape. Dedicate an area of the tank to a group of tall plants, such as straight vallis (*Vallisneria spiralis*), which will reveal the reason behind the angelfish's distinctive profile. These fish are able to swim easily through heavily vegetated areas of water, weaving between reedy plants and disappearing from would-be predators.

Colour variations

There are three types of angelfish, distinguished in part on the basis of their head shape, but these have been interbred, so most stock has hybrid origins.

Among the most commonly seen colour variants are golden strains of angelfish. Black angelfish lack the lighter silvery-brown areas found on other types. There are also angelfish with patterning and with fin variants such as in veil-tailed strains.

KEY FACTS
Family Cichlidae
Size 15cm (6in)
Water Soft, acidic
Distribution
Throughout the Amazon
Habitat Slow-flowing, well-vegetated waters
Compatibility
Peaceful
Diet Prepared foods and live foods

The blushing golden angelfish is a popular colour variant.

CONVICT CICHLID

Archocentrus nigrofasciatum

The stripes on these cichlids resemble the pattern on the traditional uniform of convicts. The fish are easy to look after, but they are aggressive, so keep pairs on their own. Females have an orange suffusion on their underparts; males often develop a slight hump on the head. As the time for spawning nears, the grey areas of their body become whiter – it's not a sign of illness.

Convict cichlids have a destructive nature. They will dig in the substrate, uprooting and eating plants. Choose tough, rapid-growing plants such as vallisneria and set them in small pots.

KEY FACTS

Family Cichlidae
Size 15cm (6in)
Water Soft and acidic
Distribution Central America, from Guatemala to Panama
Habitat Rivers and streams
Compatibility Best housed individually or as true pairs
Diet Prepared foods, live foods and greenstuff

The stripes break up the fish's outline, which hides it from potential predators.

RAM

Mikrogeophagus ramirezi

The male is larger than a female and has a bigger dorsal fin.

This delicate fish is also known as the butterfly dwarf cichlid. Male rams lack the reddish area on the underparts of females, which darkens when ready to breed. Males are territorial and aggressive towards each other – do not keep them together. The tank should be well-planted with some open stretches of water.

KEY FACTS
Family Cichlidae
Size 7.5cm (3in)
Water Soft and acidic
Distribution Rio Meta in Colombia and the Orinoco in Venezuela
Habitat Flowing water and savannah pools
Compatibility Keep individually or as pairs
Diet Prepared foods and live foods

AGASSIZ'S DWARF CICHLID

Apistogramma agassizi

Some scales on these cichlids have an appealing metallic sheen. Males can be identified by their larger size, with their caudal fin being more elongated, rather than rounded as in females. A single male can be housed with one or more females, although you will need to divide the tank with plants and rockwork to ensure that each fish has adequate space to prevent conflicts.

Good water quality is important to the well-being of these fish, so you will need to do regular partial water changes and monitor the water to keep nitrate levels low.

KEY FACTS
Family Cichlidae
Size 7.5cm (3in)
Water Soft and acidic
Distribution Tributaries of the Amazon river
Habitat River systems
Compatibility Males are likely to be combative
Diet Prepared foods and live foods

Agassiz's dwarf cichlid has a dark brown line from the tail to the eye.

FIREMOUTH CICHLID

Amphilophus macracanthus

The striking red throat of the firemouth cichlid is attractive to our eyes, but when inflated it is a threatening gesture to intimidate a potential rival, and it is also part of its courtship ritual. The red colour can be emphasized by feeding the fish a special food for enhancing fish colour.

The firemouth digs in the substrate to seek edible items and create spawning pits, where its young can be corralled after hatching to keep them safe. It is a good idea to provide them with a sandy substrate in the tank, and to set any aquarium plants in pots to prevent them being dislodged by digging.

A male has a more colourful red throat and trailing tips to its dorsal and anal fins.

KEY FACTS

Family Cichlidae
Size 15cm (6in)
Water Medium-hard and neutral
Distribution Central America, in Guatemala and Mexico
Habitat River systems
Compatibility Males are aggressive
Diet Prepared foods and live foods

LEMON CICHLID

Lamprotogus leleupi

The huge freshwater lakes of Africa's Rift Valley are home to thousands of cichlid species. The lemon cichlid found in the north-west part of Lake Tanganyika are the darkest, being orange-brown instead of yellowish. Keep pairs on their own because they are aggressive fish. The male can be recognized by his longer pelvic fins.

KEY FACTS

Family Cichlidae

Size 10cm (4in)

Water Hard and alkaline

Distribution Lake Tanganyika in East Africa

Habitat Along western and eastern shorelines

Compatibility Keep as pairs on their own

Diet Prepared foods and live foods

You can feed lemon cichlid a colour-enhancing food.

MALAWI GOLDEN CICHLID

Melanochromis auratus

The darker male Malawi golden cichlid has a blue stripe.

Only the female Malawi golden cichlid has the yellow area running underneath her body, with brown and silvery striping above. Always keep a male with several females on their own, because a single female will be persecuted, as will other fish. Provide them with plenty of retreats, and keep the tank well-lit to grow algae for the fish to eat.

KEY FACTS

Family Cichlidae
Size 12.5cm (5in)
Water Hard and alkaline
Distribution Lake Malawi in East Africa
Habitat Relatively shallow water
Compatibility Males are aggressive
Diet A prepared cichlid diet for vegetarian species

JULIE

Julidochromis ornatus

The body shape and pattern of coloration of the julie is similar to that of the female Malawi golden cichlid (see page 109). Julies from northern parts of their range have more intensive yellow underparts, compared with those from the southern area of the lake. Keep pairs on their own, and they will form a strong bond.

KEY FACTS

Family Cichlidae
Size 12.5cm (5in)
Water Hard and alkaline
Distribution Lake Tanganyika in East Africa
Habitat Relatively shallow water
Compatibility Males are aggressive
Diet Prepared cichlid food plus live foods

Mature males are slightly smaller than mature females.

WHITE-SPOTTED CICHLID

Tropheus duboisi

The spotted pattern of these cichlids fades as the fish mature. The adults themselves are variable in appearance. Those from the vicinity of the Malagarasi estuary have a wide yellow band around their bodies, while those from other areas have a white band.

White-spotted cichlids are similar in their behaviour and requirements to the mbuna cichlids in Lake Malawi, browsing on algae close to the shore. The males have longer pelvic fins than the females. They are aggressive towards each other, so keep them individually with several females.

KEY FACTS
Family Cichlidae
Size 12cm (4½in)
Water Hard and alkaline
Distribution Lake Tanganyika in East Africa
Habitat Relatively shallow water
Compatibility Males are aggressive
Diet Prepared cichlid food plus vegetable matter

The juvenile fish start off with a black coloration covered with white spots.

BREVIS

Neolamprologus brevis

These cichlids inhabit parts of the lake where snails are abundant. They do not eat the molluscs but use their shells for breeding. Design a tank for a pair of brevis with a sandy base, and add empty shells of large edible snails (*Helix* species). Females, which are a smaller size and lack an orange border at the dorsal and caudal fins, will use the shells as a retreat and for spawning.

KEY FACTS
Family Cichlidae
Size Up to 5cm (2in)
Water Hard and alkaline
Distribution Lake Tanganyika in East Africa
Habitat Sandy areas through the lake
Compatibility Keep with julies (page 110)
Diet Small prepared cichlid foods and live foods

Brevis are small and dull in colour, mainly fawn-brown.

LABIDOCHROMIS ELECTRIC YELLOW

Labidochromis caeruleus

There is tremendous variation in the colour of these cichlids, which occur in different areas around Lake Malawi. The most brightly coloured yellow specimens are from the vicinity of Kakusa, whereas the darkest deep blue examples are found in Nkhata Bay. These different morphs may be sold under various names.

Although labidochromis is a mbuna cichlid, it has a placid disposition, so you can keep it with other nonaggressive cichlids that require similar aquarium conditions. Even so, you should keep a male, recognizable by his black ventral fins, with several females.

KEY FACTS
Family Cichlidae
Size Up to 15cm (6in)
Water Hard and alkaline
Distribution Lake Malawi in East Africa
Habitat Rocky areas close to the shoreline
Compatibility Relatively tolerant in a spacious aquarium
Diet Prepared cichlid food, greenstuff and live foods

These cichlids have a black stripe on the dorsal fin that extends down the back.

KRIBENSIS

Pelvicachromis pulcher

These attractive African cichlids are easily sexed, because the female has a more vibrant purplish-red area on the belly, which explains their alternative name of purple krib. Kribensis are often found in slightly brackish waters, so the addition of a little marine salt to their aquarium water is often recommended, although not essential.

A pair of kribensis should thrive in a well-planted tank in which a flowerpot or a similar cavelike structure has been added, which the female can use as a spawning site. You can identify the sex of the fish when it is about five months old.

KEY FACTS

Family Cichlidae

Size 13cm (5¼in)

Water Soft and neutral

Distribution Coastal region of Nigeria, West Africa

Habitat Streams and slow-flowing rivers

Compatibility Territorial when breeding

Diet Prepared cichlid food, greenstuff and live foods

The female is smaller in size than the male and has a more vibrant colour.

KILLIFISH

The slender, small and often brightly coloured killifish are a fascinating group of aquarium fish, but they are not widely available through most aquatic stores.

THE COLOURFUL KILLIFISH

The patterning on killifish varies even between members of the same species, because populations have developed in isolation. Many of the African killifish have an annual life cycle, while those from Asia and the Americas spawn among plants.

The breeding cycle of the 'annual killifish' reflects their habitat of pools. These fish mature rapidly, as the water level in the pool evaporates, so they spawn in the mud at the base. The adult fish die, but the eggs remain in the mud until the rains return, when they hatch. Some fry will not emerge until the following year. If breeding killifish in a tank, expose the substrate where the eggs are laid to water at least twice.

To avoid hybridizing, keep the different species of killifish separate.

LYRETAIL

Aphyosemion australe

These killifish are named for the shape of the male's caudal fin, which is more rounded on the female. A tank for lyretail does not need to be large, but keep it covered to prevent the fish from jumping out. Keep a single male with two or three females. Or house four or five males with a dozen females. If there are only two males, one will be bullied.

KEY FACTS

Family Aplocheilidae

Size 6cm (2½in)

Water Soft and acidic

Distribution West Africa, in Gabon, Cameroon and Zaire

Habitat Rainforest pools

Compatibility Reasonably social together

Diet Prepared foods and small live foods

The male lyretail is more colourful than the female.

CLOWN KILLIFISH

Pseudepiplatys annulatus

Killifish

The fish like to hide under floating plants near the surface.

The fins of the male clown killifish are more brightly coloured than those of the female, with red markings in the caudal fin. It also has blue irises. Keep these fish in a group on their own in a tank with aquarium peat as a substrate. It maintains water conditions and mimic the darkened surroundings of their natural environment.

KEY FACTS
Family Aplocheilidae
Size 5cm (2in)
Water Soft and acidic
Distribution West Africa, in Sierra Leone, Liberia and Guinea
Habitat Rainforest pools
Compatibility Reasonably social together
Diet Prepared foods and small live foods

GÜNTHER'S NOTHOBRANCH

Nothobranchus guentheri

These are members of the so-called 'annual' killifish, and they mature quickly, within three months. Different populations of *Nothobranchus* killifish can vary quite widely in coloration, because they are frequently isolated in temporary areas of water within their natural habitat, which dry up every year until the anual rains return.

The males are aggressive, so keep a single male with several females in an aquarium, which should have a substrate of aquarium peat. These fish require relatively few plants, which is lucky as they will need plenty of open space for swimming.

Günther's nothobranch is one of the most colourful of the 'annual' killifish.

KEY FACTS

Family Aplocheilidae

Size 5cm (2in)

Water Soft and acidic

Distribution Island of Zanzibar off the coast of East Africa

Habitat Temporary pools

Compatibility Males are quarrelsome

Diet Prepared foods and small live foods

POECILIDS

Members of this group include long-time favourites such as guppies, mollies, platies and swordtails. These fish are popular simply because they are attractive, easy to keep and ideal for a community tank.

LIVE-BEARING POECILIDS

The most popular poecilids are bred in huge numbers and are far removed from their wild relatives, but breeders also work with rarer species. Because these fish are small in size, they are easy to keep in the aquarium.

Greenstuff plays an important part in the diets of many live-bearers.

These fish are all live-bearers, which mean that instead of laying eggs, like other aquarium fish, they give birth to live young. If you keep the fry out of reach of adult fish, they are easier to rear than the young of egg-laying species, thanks to the fry's larger size. You can feed them tiny pieces of flaked food, crumbled through the fingers to form a powder.

GUPPY

Poecilia reticulata

Guppies have been developed in a striking array of colours and patterns, far removed from their wild ancestors. A group of guppies makes an impressive display together, but you can keep them with other nonaggressive fish as part of a community aquarium. However, do not mix those with elaborate fins with fish that are likely to be fin-nippers such as barbs.

Aside from the different colour varieties, which can range from shades of yellow to red, green and blue, there are a number of guppies with striking patterns such as the cobra guppy. The caudal fin may be a rounded or delta shape, a swordtail with a longer projection or even a lyretail with projections top and bottom; most swordtail and lyretail guppies

The female is larger in size and less colourful than the male.

This blonde red guppy is one of the many colour variations available.

KEY FACTS

Family Poeciliidae
Size 5cm (2in)
Water Relatively hard and alkaline
Distribution Central and northern South America, and the Caribbean
Habitat Ditches to lakes and rivers
Compatibility Not aggressive
Diet Prepared foods, greenstuff and small live foods

have a dorsal fin with a long, pointed shape.

Guppies are easy to sex because, like many live-bearers, the anal fin of the male fish has developed into a rodlike feature known as the gonopodium. This is used to transfer sperm into the female's body during mating. Guppies are prolific fish, but they have a short lifespan of a year. If you purchase adult fish, they will only live for a few months.

The green cobra guppy has a snakelike pattern on its body and most of its fins.

PLATY

Xiphophorus maculatus

There are many different varieties of the platy, based on modifications to the coloration, fin shape and patterning of these fish. These varieties have arisen in part thanks to natural variations seen within platy populations in the wild, and these have been combined to create the domesticated strains that are available today. Platies are sometimes known as moonfish because of the presence of a black marking at the base of the caudal fin, which resembles the shape of a crescent-shaped moon.

Sexing is straightforward on the basis of the size of the fish, with the females growing almost twice as large as males. The females also have an anal fin, instead of the narrow, tubelike gonopodium found on the males, which is used for mating. (Because these fish are live-bearers, fertilization takes place internally.)

Caring for the fish

The blue coral platy has a blue spot near the marks on its caudal peduncle.

Platies normally inhabit shallow stretches of water in the wild, which warm up quickly when they receive sunlight. Because these fish are

The pigmentation on the black platy is variable.

often exposed to relatively higher temperatures, they will appreciate a water temperature of 25°C (77°F) in the aquarium. The other effect of the sunlight is to encourage algal growth in these surroundings, so platies will browse on plant matter in the aquarium. Make sure you offer these fish greenstuff as part of their diet on a regular basis.

KEY FACTS
Family Poeciliidae
Size 6cm (2½in)
Water Relatively hard and alkaline
Distribution Central America
Habitat Standing water such as pools and marshes
Compatibility Not aggressive
Diet Prepared foods, greenstuff and small live foods

SWORDTAIL

Xiphophorus helleri

These fish are so-called because of the long, swordlike projection on the lower edge of the caudal fin of the male. The females are a larger size, and mature females sometimes develop an extension on their caudal fin. Swordtails often inhabit fast-flowing water in the wild, so they prefer well-oxygenated water.

There are a number of closely related species or subspecies of swordtail. Bright coloration can be found on the pineapple swordtail and the gold swordtail. The males of strains have a corresponding extension to the upper tip of their caudal fin.

Aggressive males

Male swordtails are often aggressive. You can keep a male with two or three females, but do not do so with

The colour of the green swordtail is reminiscent of wild fish.

The female normally lacks the swordlike projection.

another male, as the weaker male will be bullied. To keep males without fighting, house them in a large tank with six to ten other species – the males will not come into contact so often.

You should avoid housing swordtails with fish such as barbs, which can damage their swordlike extensions. Also avoid keeping swordtails with platies, because they can breed, creating hybrid offspring.

KEY FACTS
Family Poeciliidae
Size 10cm (4in)
Water Relatively hard and alkaline
Distribution The eastern side of Central America
Habitat Fast-flowing waters, with plenty of vegetation
Compatibility Males can be extremely quarrelsome
Diet Prepared foods and small live foods

MOLLY

Poecilia velifera

Females are larger than males and have a normal anal fin.

There are a number of different mollies, which are distinguished by the fish's enlarged dorsal fin – it is often likened to a sail on the top of their bodies. Their attractive matt, velvet-like appearance has made black mollies immensely popular. Colour variations include mollies with contrasting silvery and black patterning, as well as marbled individuals. Brighter shades include the so-called marmalade, with its predominantly orange coloration. Lyretailed variants have also been bred in these different colours.

The balloon molly has a modified shape, which includes a naturally swollen belly. Lacking the naturally elegant profile of the sailfin itself, the balloon molly can be cumbersome when swimming.

Caring for mollies

Mollies need slightly brackish water, and they are vulnerable to fungus and white spot (see page 162) if their surroundings are less than optimal. If keeping sailfish mollies and balloon mollies in an aquarium together, check there is enough food. Otherwise, the sailfin mollies may take the majority of the food available. Mollies will seek natural food in the tank such as algae. If algae is in short supply, the fish will nibble on aquarium plants. Only tough plants such as vallisneria should be planted in the tank.

KEY FACTS

Family Poeciliidae

Size 18cm (7¼in)

Water Relatively hard and alkaline

Distribution Originally from Mexico's Yucatán peninsula

Habitat Brackish waters, with plenty of vegetation

Compatibility Reasonably social, but males may disagree

Diet Prepared foods, greenstuff and small live foods

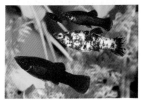

Black mollies are common, but other types include black and silver mollies.

CYPRINIDS

The cyprinids represent the largest group of freshwater fish and contain many popular species such as danios, barbs and rasboras. The goldfish is the most popular pet fish in the world.

Barbs can be aggressive, and they are likely to nip long, trailing fins of slower swimming fish.

THE ACTIVE CYPRINIDS

Cyprinids are active, shoaling fish. In most cases you should keep them in groups, but there are exceptions, as in the case of the red-tailed black shark (see page 134). Not all cyprinids need heated surroundings, but many need water filtered through aquarium peat.

The popular cyprinids are bred commercially on a huge scale, which has led to many colour and fin variants. However, breeding them in the home tank is difficult because they eat their eggs. You will need to set up a spawning tank, and the fry require special foods until they can eat powdered flaked food.

WHITE CLOUD MOUNTAIN MINNOW

Tanichthys albonubes

This attractive fish is a cyprinid that will thrive in a tank at room temperature. However, it needs good water circulation and frequent partial water changes to reflect the conditions in its natural habitat of fast-flowing streams.

These fish will look best in a group. You should buy them together rather than from different sources – otherwise, they may be reluctant to integrate into a shoal. There are two different colour variants (red and yellow), plus a long-finned strain. Adult females are slightly smaller than males.

KEY FACTS

Family Cyprinidae

Size 4cm (1½in)

Water Relatively soft and acidic, but adaptable

Distribution Area of Canton, China

Habitat Fast-flowing, cool mountain streams

Compatibility Lives in groups

Diet Prepared foods, greenstuff and live foods

White Cloud Mountain minnows from Hong Kong have red edges on its fins.

GOLDFISH

Carassius auratus

The traditional goldfish is orange with a slim body.

The goldfish can be remarkably long-lived – they have been known to live as long as 40 years. There are many types of goldfish, differing not just in their coloration but also in their physical appearance. Until recently, many strains remained localized to their area of development.

Types of goldfish

The traditional goldfish is a fish with a slim body and compact fins, including a powerful caudal fin. They are often orange-red in colour, but they can also be a variable golden shade. Bi-coloured orange and white goldfish with individual patterns are common. Pure white goldfish are also seen occasionally.

Another popular group of goldfish are the shubunkins. These have a mottled appearance, with a variable depth of blue coloration on their bodies, ranging from light blue to a violet shade. Orange and whitish markings are sometimes apparent.

The 'fancy' breeds of goldfish have a shorter, more compact body shape. This group includes the lionhead and the oranda, both of which develop a swelling, known as a hood, or wen, on their head as they mature. The lionhead lacks a dorsal fin in the centre of its back. Both can be brightly coloured, but darker varieties include a steely-blue and a chocolate form of the oranda.

KEY FACTS

Family Cyprinidae

Size 25cm (10in) or more

Water Relatively soft and acidic, but adaptable

Distribution Southern China

Habitat Sluggish rivers

Compatibility Gets along well with other fish

Diet Prepared foods, greenstuff and live foods

The lionhead goldfish does not have a dorsal fin on its back.

The darkest goldfish is the moor, which is blackish with lighter underparts. The eyes of some moors protrude – they are known as telescopic-eyed. Celestial goldfish have eyes that look permanently upwards, with fleshy growths on the sides. Bubble-eyes have an even more distinctive appearance, with large sacs under their eyes. These goldfish need a clear area of water in the aquarium, without rocks that could puncture the sacs.

It is difficult to sex goldfish outside the spawning period, although when viewed from above, females may have broader and longer bodies. As spawning approaches, males develop white pimples on their gill plates, behind the eyes, which extend along the top

The red-capped oranda has double anal and caudal fins.

The pearlscale goldfish has a pearly coloured raised area on each scale.

of the pectoral fins. There is usually disturbance within the tank as the males chase the females.

Caring for goldfish

Goldfish are easy to keep in an unheated aqarium, but it should be large because these fish can grow fast. The tank will need a good filtration system to keep the water clean. An undergravel filter is recommended, but also incorporate a power filter.

The fish will dig in the base of the tank, so plant only hardy plants such as Canadian pondweed (*Elodea canadensis*). Make sure they are well-supported if you do not want them to be constantly uprooted. Feeding is easy, and you can tame goldfish to come up and feed from your hand, using either flake or pellet foods. Special diets are available for some of the fancy varieties such as the oranda.

This young bubble-eye goldfish has fluid-filled swellings under its eyes.

RED-TAILED BLACK SHARK

Epalzeorhynchos bicolor

The shape of this cyprinid and its red, forked tail explains its common name, although it is not related to sharks. The red-tailed black shark must be kept apart from others of its own kind, including related species, because it is highly territorial. A suitable environment for these fish must include adequate retreats, with a soft, sandy substrate. The tank should also be well-planted to provide good cover.

In an established aquarium, these fish will browse on algae, in addition to taking other food, which should include some greenstuff such as lettuce and flakes.

The red-tailed black shark has a high dorsal fin and a streamlined body.

KEY FACTS

Family Cyprinidae

Size 15cm (6in)

Water Relatively soft and acidic

Distribution Thailand in south-east Asia

Habitat Rivers

Compatibility Does not get along with its own kind

Diet Prepared foods, including flake, plus fresh greenstuff

MOSQUITO RASBORA

Boraras brigittae

KEY FACTS
Family Cyprinidae
Size 3.5cm (1½in)
Water Relatively soft and acidic
Distribution Parts of Indonesia and southern Borneo
Habitat Small pools, slow-flowing streams
Compatibility Lives in groups
Diet Prepared foods and live foods

These tiny rasboras are easy to manage and will thrive if you keep them together in a shoal. You can also mix them alongside other non-aggressive companions. Their small size makes them an ideal choice for a small aquarium. These rasbora prefer relatively shaded conditions, complete with floating plants at the surface of the water.

Males are usually more brightly coloured than females.

HARLEQUIN RASBORA
Trigonostigma heteromorpha

Harlequins have a triangular marking on their flanks. Like others in the group, these fish require water filtered through aquarium peat. Keep them in shoals. Set up well-planted areas, including floating plants for subdued lighting, and open spaces where the fish can congregate. Females have a broader profile from the side than males.

KEY FACTS

Family Cyprinidae
Size 5cm (2in)
Water Relatively soft and acidic
Distribution Parts of Thailand, Malaysia and Sumatra
Habitat Slow-flowing, often shady streams
Compatibility Strong shoaling instincts
Diet Prepared foods and live foods

The true harlequin rasbora has a silvery hue to its body.

SCISSORTAIL RASBORA

Rasbora trilineata

The upper and lower parts of the tail have dark tips.

As the scissortail rasbora swims forwards, the gap between the lobes of its tail close like the blades of a scissor. The species is also called the three-lined rasbora, due to the dark stripes along the sides of its body. This rasbora can swim fast, so make sure the tank has open areas. Sexing can be difficult, but females may have a more rounded body than males.

KEY FACTS

Family Cyprinidae
Size 10cm (4in)
Water Relatively soft and acidic
Distribution Parts of Thailand, Malaysia, Sumatra and Borneo
Habitat Slow-flowing, often shady streams
Compatibility Strong shoaling instincts
Diet Prepared food and live foods

ZEBRA DANIO

Danio rerio

Both sexes have two pairs of tiny barbels near the mouth.

The alternating blue and light yellowish stripes of zebra danios suggest their common name. Females are slightly larger than males, with a more rounded body. These danios are easy to care for and are attractive in a shoal. They tend to swim near the surface of the tank. Keep the aquarium covered at all times to prevent the fish from leaping out.

KEY FACTS
Family Cyprinidae
Size 5cm (2in)
Water Relatively soft and acidic
Distribution Parts of Bangladesh and eastern India
Habitat Slow-flowing stretches of water
Compatibility Strong shoaling instincts
Diet Prepared foods and live foods

GREAT DANIO

Devario aequipinnatus

These danios can grow large, but you can keep them in a community tank. They are active and prefer to swim in the upper part of the tank. They have individual markings that help to identify the fish. Females have broader bodies than males. The central blue stripe in female fish is slightly upturned on the caudal fin.

KEY FACTS

Family Cyprinidae
Size 15cm (6in)
Water Relatively soft and acidic
Distribution Sri Lanka and western India
Habitat Slow-flowing stretches of water
Compatibility Strong shoaling instincts
Diet Prepared foods and live foods

The yellow stripes and blue bands extend along the body.

ROSY BARB

Barbus conchonius

These barbs are adaptable, and a shoal swimming in open areas is attractive in an aquarium. There is also a long-finned form available. Females have a more rotund body shape than males.

These fish need a well-planted area in the tank. However, they can be disruptive fish, particularly if housed with smaller companions, and they like to dig in the substrate. Make sure you weigh down the plants to prevent them from floating to the surface. These barbs can normally thrive in even medium-hard water conditions, but they will need soft-water surroundings when breeding.

KEY FACTS

Family Cyprinidae

Size 12.5cm (5in)

Water Relatively soft and neutral

Distribution North-eastern parts of India

Habitat Slow-flowing stretches of water

Compatibility Strong shoaling instincts

Diet Prepared foods, greenstuff and live foods

The reddish coloration is more pronounced in males when ready to spawn.

TIGER BARB

Barbus tetrazona

These barbs can be more aggressive than related species and cannot be trusted alongside fish with long, flowing fins in a community tank because they often nibble at their fins. However, such is the popularity of the tiger barb, which has vertical black bands on its body, that there are now several different colour variants. They include the red tiger barb, which has an overall reddish coloration without the dark banding. There is also a green variety, sometimes called the moss-banded. Always check the entire tank of tiger barbs before buying any. They are susceptible to white spot (see page 162).

KEY FACTS
Family Cyprinidae
Size 7cm (2¾in)
Water Relatively soft and slightly acidic
Distribution Southeast Asia, including Sumatra and Borneo
Habitat Slow-flowing stretches of water
Compatibility Strong shoaling instincts
Diet Prepared foods, greenstuff and live foods

The striped tiger barb, like others in this group, prefers to be kept in a shoal.

TINFOIL BARB

Barbus schwanefeldi

These barbs will reach a large size, so they are not suitable for a community tank. They will outgrow their companions and may even prey on them. Tinfoil barbs look spectacular in a large tank with non-aggressive species such as some of the larger catfish or cichlids that require similar water conditions. Keep tinfoil barbs in small shoals, because a fish kept on his own will be nervous and hide. The young are less colourful than the adults, without the dark markings on the fins. Include some robust plants in the tank set in small pots, as these cyprinids eat vegetation and dig in the substrate.

KEY FACTS
Family Cyprinidae
Size 35cm (14in)
Water Relatively soft and slightly acidic
Distribution South-east Asia
Habitat Slow-flowing stretches of water
Compatibility Strong shoaling instincts
Diet Prepared foods, greenstuff and live foods

The more common variety of the tinfoil barb has a silver body.

SIAMESE FLYING FOX

Crossocheilus siamensis

The Siamese flying fox prefers the base of the tank.

KEY FACTS
Family Cyprinidae
Size 15cm (6in)
Water Relatively soft and slightly acidic
Distribution South-east Asia, Thailand and Malayasia
Habitat Streams
Compatibility Best to keep apart from its own kind
Diet Greenstuff and live foods

The Siamese flying fox is a useful fish for browsing on algae – it will even nibble on thread algae, which can clog up the leaves of other plants. This fish is relatively shy, so there must be well-planted areas in the aquarium that can serve as retreats for the fish. It is also territorial, so keep only one in the tank. The fish will need a tank that is well-oxygenated.

MISCELLANEOUS FISH

There are many other types of fish, from the burrowing wormlike loaches to the flat-backed butterflyfish. There are also new varieties available.

ESTABLISHING NEW BREEDS

New varieties occur when a collector obtains some initial breeding stock, and the offspring of these fish are passed to experienced fish-keepers. They then turn up in specialized aquatic outlets, before becoming generally available. With any fish, never buy one without knowing what it is – you will not be able to care for it properly, and it could outgrow the tank.

By keeping unusual fish you can add to the existing knowledge about the species. Record your observations on the breeding attempts of the fish – whether they are ultimately successful or not – and you can post this information on bulletin boards for fellow enthusiasts.

The rainbowfish is one group that has grown in popularity in recent years.

COOLIE LOACH

Acanthophthalmus kuhlii

The coolie loach is secretive and usually hides during the day among rockwork and other tank decor. They like to burrow in a soft sandy substrate. If you need to catch a coolie loach, do so carefully. It will retreat into inaccessible areas, and it also has small spines beneath each eye, which can be caught in the net. Make sure you free it from a net gently.

KEY FACTS
Family Cobitidae
Size 10cm (4in)
Water Relatively soft and slightly acidic
Distribution Malay Peninsula and parts of Indonesia
Habitat Slow-flowing, soft-bottomed waters
Compatibility Strong shoaling instincts
Diet Food tablets and wormlike live foods

The pattern of the banding varies in the coolie loach.

CLOWN LOACH

Botia macracanthus

The colourful clown loach, which is active during the day, can grow large enough to prey on smaller fish. This loach rests at a strange angle in the water, with its body tilted. There is no need for concern as this is normal for the fish. It digs in the substrate, so include sandy areas in the tank, and also add bogwood and rockwork to provide retreats.

KEY FACTS

Family Cobitidae
Size 30cm (12in)
Water Soft, acidic
Distribution Indonesia, notably Sumatra, and Borneo
Habitat Well-oxygenated, soft-bottomed streams
Compatibility Aggressive when older
Diet Food tablets and wormlike live foods

The stripes have given the fish another name – tiger loach.

LAKE KUTUBU RAINBOWFISH

Melanotaenia lacustris

The bluish shades on the flanks of the Lake Kutubu rainbowfish vary in their depth of colour. The water conditions and lighting can have an influence too.

The bluish coloration is most prominent in mature males.

These rainbowfish will require a lower water temperature of 22–25°C (72–77°F). They will also benefit from a large expanse of open water for swimming. Lake Kutubu rainbowfish shoal close to the water's surface, so offer them flake food, which floats at the surface. These fish also eat plants such as duckweed (*Lemna* sp.). The duckweed will also help to diffuse the level of illumination in the tank, which will improve the coloration of the fish.

KEY FACTS

Family Melanotaeniidae

Size 12cm (4¾in)

Water Hard and alkaline

Distribution Southern highlands of New Guinea

Habitat Lake Kutubu and the Soro River

Compatibility Social

Diet Prepared foods and live foods

ELEPHANT-NOSED FISH

Gnathonemus petersii

This unusual fish prefers a fine, sandy substrate where it can dig for worms. Make sure the tank is also well-planted to provide cover. The fish has an electrical organ that produces pulses for orientation purposes, so avoid keeping these and related mormyrids together. The electrical discharges will upset their companions.

KEY FACTS

Family Mormyridae

Size 23cm (9in)

Water Relatively soft and acidic

Distribution Western and central Africa

Habitat River drainage systems

Compatibility Not aggressive towards unrelated species

Diet Prefers live foods

It is difficult to get the fish to take food other than worms.

AFRICAN KNIFEFISH *Xenomystus nigri*

The anal and caudal fins of the African knifefish are fused together, running along the underside of the body to create a wavy appendage that extends to the tip of the tail, with the anal fin itself close to the head. Knifefish can gulp down air from the atmosphere. They may make unusual sounds, which are the result of air passing out of the swim bladder. The fish is territorial, so keep only one in a tank.

KEY FACTS
Family Notopteridae
Size 20cm (8in)
Water Relatively soft and acidic
Distribution From West Africa, in the Niger River
Habitat Rivers and associated waterways
Compatibility Antisocial towards its own kind
Diet Generally prefers live foods, especially small worms

Set up a well-planted tank with a fine, sandy substrate. The fish is more active at dusk and prefers floating plants at the surface to diffuse the lighting.

This African knifefish has an electrical organ, which it uses to orientate itself.

BUTTERFLYFISH

Pantodon buchholzi

The butterflyfish can use their pectoral fins to propel themselves out of the water. Hence the reason to keep the tank covered as much as possible, even when maintaining the tank.

KEY FACTS
Family Pantodontidae
Size 4cm (1½in)
Water Soft, acidic
Distribution Eastern Peru, South America
Habitat Shaded waters
Compatibility Peaceful, shoaling
Diet Prefers live foods

Butterflyfish swim at the surface, so include floating plants in the tank. These fish are ambush predators, hiding under vegetation and leaping out to grab passing invertebrates. They are compatible in a small group together, but do not keep them with other surface-dwellers, such as hatchetfish (see page 96).

The fish can use its broad pectoral fins like wings to glide.

INDIAN GLASSFISH

Chanda ranga

Glassfish are so-called because of their transparent bodies. Keep Indian glassfish, which live in brackish water, in a small shoal, as they have a nervous nature. When purchasing fish, check the water conditions in which they are being kept, and replicate them in your tank. Mix marine salt in with fresh water, following the instructions on the packaging, to create a solution of the correct strength. This helps the fish to acclimatize after the move; then you can make any changes gradually as required. Do not buy fish with vivid green or red coloration. A disreputable dealer will have injected them with a harmful dye.

KEY FACTS

Family Ambassidae

Size 7.5cm (3in)

Water Hard and slightly alkaline

Distribution Asia, from India east to Thailand

Habitat Often found in estuaries

Compatibility Nervous yet peaceful

Diet Prefers live foods, but it may also eat flaked foods

The Indian glassfish has a elongated body shape and a greenish-golden tint.

BUMBLEBEE GOBY

Brachygobius xanthozonus

Many gobies are found in the marine environment, where their ventral fins form a suction cup that helps them to anchor on to rocks in turbulent water. However, some species such as the bumblebee goby are found in brackish water.

You can keep these gobies in a relatively small aquarium, but they are best accommodated on their own. Because they are nervous by nature, they are at a disadvantage when obtaining food alongside bolder fish. A tank setup for bumblebee gobies will need bogwood and rockwork to provide retreats, plus a few plants that thrive in brackish water such as cryptocornes.

KEY FACTS
Family Gobiidae
Size 5cm (2in)
Water Hard and slightly alkaline
Distribution Sumatra, Java and Borneo
Habitat Often found in estuaries
Compatibility Territorial and timid
Diet Prepared foods and live foods

Males are more brightly coloured, while females have a stockier profile.

GREEN PUFFERFISH

Tetraodon fluviatilis

Pufferfish can inflate their bodies to anchor themselves in a tight space if being attacked. This fish needs brackish surroundings, and plastic plants will be ideal to create dense cover. Young pufferfish are compatible, but they become aggressive towards each other as they grow older.

Do not add aquatic snails to a tank with pufferfish if you do not want the fish to prey on them. Instead, offer pufferfish pieces of prawn in their shells, which can help to wear down their teeth. If the teeth become overgrown, the fish will have difficulty eating.

KEY FACTS

Family Tetraodontidae
Size 15cm (6in)
Water Hard and slightly alkaline
Distribution South-east Asia to the Philippines
Habitat Often found in estuaries
Compatibility Rather aggressive
Diet Primarily eats live foods

Pufferfish have four teeth, two on each jaw, which can become overgrown.

KEEPING YOUR FISH HEALTHY

When diseases do strike, they can usually be traced back to environmental problems. Feeding your fish correctly is important because giving them too much food is often the cause of these problems.

FOODS AND FEEDING

Most fish are opportunistic in their feeding habits, so they can be easily persuaded to eat specially formulated foods. Feed your fish a variety of foods, including live foods, to help ensure they stay healthy.

It may be difficult at first, but you'll need to discover roughly how much food your fish will eat. If you feed your fish too much food, it will go uneaten and pollute the water, which can lead to disease.

Regular meals

Most fish feed frequently and should be given food several times each day. For nocturnal species, feed them at dusk and again just before you go to bed, when they will be most

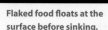

Flaked food floats at the surface before sinking.

active. Some feeding guidelines are given on the fish food. Use these as a starting point, and aim to provide no more than the fish will eat within five minutes.

If you feed your fish three or four times in the day, vary the food you offer them. You can provide a dried food, then augment it with a live food. Freeze-dried is the easiest option, or give your fish frozen or live foods.

Commercial foods

The bulk of the diet consists of specially formulated foods. They are inexpensive, and the fish eat only small quantities. An increasing number of foods are available in aquatic stores, from general-purpose products for all the fish in a community tank to specialist diets for particular groups of fish such as guppies, discus and goldfish. There are even some that help enhance a fish's colour.

Flaked foods

Many prepared dried foods are made in flake form, which has a thin, wafer-like appearance. Flaked food will float at the surface of the water for a while, so it is ideal for fish that feed in this area of water. It is also

Flaked food is an easy way of feeding most fish.

useful for young fish. However, flaked foods tend to be nibbled at, and uneaten food will sink to the substrate, where it can pollute the water.

Pellets and other solid forms

There are pellets and tablets of different shapes. Pellets are usually eaten whole, which helps to

prevent wastage. You should match the size of the fish to that of the pellet. If in doubt, opt for a smaller size of pellet that the fish will be able to swallow easily. Catfish pellets have a denser texture than goldfish pellets, and are designed to sink rapidly to the base of the tank, making them ideal for bottom-dwellers such as corydoras. Try to drop

Large tablets are an option for feeding catfish.

these pellets so they fall into a clear area. If they land out of reach, in a crevice between rocks, for example, the pellets will pollute the water.

Other forms of food suitable for larger fish such as cichlids and goldfish are foodsticks. They are sucked into the fish's mouth lengthwise.

Supplementary dry foods

A range of other dried foods is also available, which can be a useful supplement to a diet. They include spirulina, a nutritious form of algae eaten by many fish, which may also help to improve their coloration.

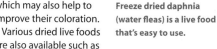

Freeze dried daphnia (water fleas) is a live food that's easy to use.

Various dried live foods are available such as daphnia (water fleas) and tubificid worms, as well as river shrimp, which are suitable for bigger fish with predatory feeding habits.

In a freeze-dried form, these foods retain their nutritional value and yet can be stored easily, without having to be refrigerated. They also reduce the risk of introducing disease to the tank. Some foods such as tubificid worms are sold as blocks that are dropped into the water – the fish dart up to nibble off pieces.

Frozen foods and live foods

You need to store frozen foods, which are usually supplied in small packs, in the freezer and thaw a block just before feeding it to the fish. If you don't use

River shrimp are a treat for larger fish, whether freeze-dried or as a live food.

a whole block, shave off some small sections carefully with a sharp knife. These will thaw quickly at room temperature. Frozen food is usually more palatable than freeze-dried food because it has a higher water content, making it more like natural live foods.

Live foods

Although live foods are available from aquatic stores, they can introduce disease to the tank. If you want to offer invertebrates to the fish, the safest option is to cultivate them yourself.

Some fish-keepers prefer to cultivate daphnia in a spare aquarium. Simply remove some with a sieve as required. You can obtain bloodworm, another popular live food, in the summer months by leaving out a bucket of water, where midges can lay their eggs. These hatch into bloodworms, so-called because of their colour.

Other live foods include terrestrial foods such as hatchling crickets (*Gryllus domesticus*) and wingless fruit flies (*Drosophila*), sold for reptiles and amphibians, are used to supplement the diets of some fish. These are not essential to the well-being of most common aquarium fish.

Feeding the vegetarians

As far as the more vegetarian species are concerned, there is no reason why you cannot provide them with fresh items to supplement their regular diet. Slices of courgette or cucumber, for example, are a favourite of many loricariid catfish. Ideally, use organic vegetables if possible. You will need to remove any left uneaten before the end of the day with a net, so only offer a single slice at a time.

Catfish are fond of courgettes and cucumber, and these also have taken a liking to slices of potato.

DISEASES

There are many ways in which diseases can be introduced to an aquarium. By knowing how they occur you will be better prepared to prevent them – or treat them successfully in the event of an outbreak.

How diseases occur

Introducing a sick fish into an aquarium is one way of spreading disease, but it is not the only one. Harmful microbes may be in the water in which the fish are transported from the store, which is why it is not a good idea to empty the fish with the water into the tank (see pages 54–59).

In a typical aquarium, there are organisms that can cause infection, but these usually do not have the

The fins on guppies are susceptible to nips from other fish. Fin damage can be followed by fungal infection.

opportunity because the fish's immune system is able to fight off these microbes. However, if the fish's body is injured, infections such as fungal disease will have an opportunity to attack.

The role of stress

Stress also plays a part in disease, and this helps to explain why fish often become ill following a move, which is generally one of the most stressful times for a fish. Similarly, a fish that is repeatedly bullied in a tank will probably develop minor scale damage, which will leave the fish susceptible to fungal attack.

A power cut

Tropical fish can become ill if they are chilled. If the power goes off, unplug the lights and cover the tank with a duvet to retain heat. When the power is restored, you should allow the temperature to rise gradually and remove the duvet before reconnecting the lights. Keep an eye on the fish for a few days.

Keeping a separate tank

The sooner that the signs of illness are observed and the quicker you take action, the easier it will be to treat the fish successfully. You can invest in a small, lightweight acrylic tank to use as a 'hospital' tank to isolate and treat sick individuals. It can also serve as a quarantine tank to house new fish before introducing them to the established tank.

Newcomers to the main tank need to integrate with the existing fish, and this is often stressful at first. If you have kept and fed them well for a two weeks beforehand, health problems are less likely to arise.

Symptoms and diseases

Always check the fish in the tank every day for signs of illness. Begin any necessary treatment as soon as possible to lessen the risk of secondary infections.

If most of the fish in the tank die suddenly, suspect environmental factors such as a spray. Avoid using sprays near the tank – many are deadly to fish.

Parasites and fungus

White spot: Tiny white spots appear over the fish's body. These ulcerate, releasing microscopic infective tomites to attack other susceptible fish. An affected fish is at risk of fungal attack. White spot spreads by water from one tank to another. *Use a proprietary remedy to destroy the tomites and watch for signs of fungus.* Common.

Velvet disease: Most often occurs in

Don't buy a bloated fish, and never buy fish from a tank with white spot.

anabantoids. The disease causes the fish's body colour to become yellowish-grey. The fish will rub itself to relieve irritation and may show signs of breathing difficulty.

Treat with a proprietary remedy.
Relatively common.

Flukes: These attach to the skin or, less conspicuously, in the gills, resulting in laboured gill movements.

Proprietary treatments are available, but there is a possibility of reinfection.
Relatively common.

Hole-in-the-Head: This is most likely to occur in discus, but it can also strike other fish. Whitish spots appear on the head and start to ulcerate. Secondary infection can occur.

Don't buy any fish with clamped fins such as on this platy, a sign of gill fluke.

Treatment with a drug called miconazole gives the best hope of recovery. Fish that recover may have scarring.
Relatively common.

Saprolegnia fungus: An infection that strikes after an injury, causing a white haloed effect over the affected area. Infective spores are in the water.

It can be treated with a cream carefully applied to the affected area, or by baths with a proprietary remedy.

Improve the water quality, and raise the temperature slightly to improve the fish's immune response.
Common.

Bacterial

Fin rot: This often strikes following damage to the fins and results in reddening of the damaged areas. The risk is greatest if the water quality is poor. There is also a serious risk of secondary fungal infection. *Treat the fish with a proprietary remedy.*
Common.

Mouth fungus: Guppies and other live-bearers are the most vulnerable fish. The fungus causes an unpleasant cottonwool-like growth in the mouth, preventing the fish from eating – the fish will show signs of weight loss.
It can be treated with an antibiotic bath. Carry out a partial water change in the main aquarium.
Less common.

Vibriosis: There are several serious, generalized signs of infection, including reddening of the body, changes in colour and swollen abdomen and eyes. It attacks rapidly and is fatal, and it spreads quickly through an aquarium.
It is hard to treat, but antibiotics may help.
Less common.

Piscine tuberculosis: There is a chronic loss of weight and colour, and the eyes may protrude abnormally.

There will be widespread losses in the aquarium.
Note: Piscine tuberculosis can cause a skin infection in
people, but it does not attack the respiratory system.
*No treatment possible. Strip down the tank, disinfect it
and then restock it.*
Less common.

Viral

Lymphocystis: Most likely to be seen in goldfish, but
it can strike other fish too. Isolated white nodules will
form on the body surface. It is disfiguring but causes
the fish little discomfort.
Treatment is not really possible.
Common.

Malawi bloat: A problem that affects cichlids from
Lake Malawi, especially vegetarian species. The
abdomen becomes swollen and the eyes may
protrude – a condition referred to as exophthalmia.
It may be caused by a viral infection, possibly
associated with a lack of fibre in the fish's diet.
*No direct treatment is possible, but adding fibre to the
fish's diet may help.*
Less common.

Iridiovirus: Body colour of affected fish darkens
noticeably, with the abdomen swelling. It affects
many fish.
No treatment possible.
Less common.

BREEDING

Breeding fish in the home can provide an intriguing new aspect to keeping fish. While some fish will breed readily, others present a much greater challenge. If you are hoping to breed your fish, be prepared to invest in another tank and further equipment. It is also important to think about how you will find homes for the extra fish, because some pairs can produce amazingly large numbers of offspring.

BREEDING BEHAVIOUR

Fish have a number of different breeding strategies, but they can be divided into live-bearing and egg-laying fish. Look out for signs of breeding behaviour – there are also measures you can take to encourage breeding.

Live-bearers

As their name suggests, live-bearing fish give birth to live young, although there is often no direct connection internally between the body of the female and

A male live-bearer fertilizes a female internally.

The eggs of egg-laying fish tend to drift down among plants, or they may be swept away on currents.

her offspring developing inside her. The eggs may be retained in her body, and the young hatch as they are born. Live-bearers display no parental instincts, which means that their young are at risk of being eaten from the moment of birth.

Egg-layers

Many egg-laying fish are dedicated parents. Various male anabantoids build special nests for their eggs and guard their young when they hatch. Others such as angelfish carefully deposit their eggs and remain in the vicinity of their nest site until the fry emerge, which they will then try to keep safe from predators.

In certain species, the parent fish take the eggs into their mouth – this is known as mouth-brooding. They retain the eggs without feeding until the young emerge up to three weeks later. Such behaviour is seen in bettas and cichlids and a few catfish.

A few fish bury their eggs to protect them. Such behaviour is seen in annual killifish, whose natural habitat of temporary pools dries up, leaving the adult fish to die. Safely entombing their eggs in mud until the rains return allows the next generation to hatch. However, most egg-laying fish scatter their eggs at random. Fish such as barbs and tetras lay large numbers of eggs because in the wild few survive.

Ready for breeding

Signs of breeding behaviour are usually clear-cut. The male fish often pursues the female fish more actively and their coloration often becomes brighter than normal. Females will swell up with their eggs or offspring, with certain specific signs such as the appearance of a black spot on some live-bearers indicating that a brood is soon on the way.

Stimulating breeding behaviour

A number of triggers can encourage breeding. They include adjusting the water temperature slightly in certain cases, while carrying out more frequent partial water changes to mimic the effect of the rains, which can encourage breeding in some fish in the wild. Increasing the amount of live food in the diet can also have a similar

For most egg-laying fish, the males fertilize the eggs as they are laid by the females.

effect. Certain species of live-bearers such as guppies are much easier to condition for breeding purposes than others, provided that environmental conditions are favourable.

Anabantoids

While some of the rare bettas are mouth-brooders (see pages 167–68), the most commonly kept species such as the gouramis and the Siamese fighting fish are egg-layers. A spawning tank for egg-laying anabantoids should have a low water level, some vegetation floating at the top of the tank and a gentle filtration system. Otherwise, the delicate bubble nest, which the male makes with his saliva, will be destroyed.

After spawning occurs, remove the female to prevent her from being attacked by the male, who guards the nest until the young hatch several days later. At this point remove the male too.

Young anabantoids have small mouths, so at first provide them with fine particles of food. Their labyrinth organs, which allow them to breathe atmospheric air, only begin to function once they are about three weeks old. You should separate the young males once they are about two months of age,

The male Siamese fighting fish carries the eggs laid by the female to its bubble nest after each batch is spawned.

when they can be sexed, to prevent them from fighting ferociously with each other.

Catfish

It is usually only the smaller species of catfish that breed in tank surroundings. One of the difficulties is being able to distinguish between the sexes of these fish to be sure that you have a pair. However, because the corydoras catfish can be kept in small groups, this is not always an obstacle.

It may be possible to trigger spawning in some of the Amazonian species by carrying out a partial water change in the tank, dropping the water temperature slightly and increasing the amount of live food in the diet. This mimics the changes in their natural habitat, where spawning normally occur after heavy rains. In the case of corydoras catfish, eggs will be laid on aquatic plants. Some types such as the banjo catfish are substrate spawners. The male digs a spawning pit for the eggs and watches over them until they hatch.

Keep small catfish in a small group if you want a pair to match up and breed.

Characiforms

Specific water conditions are required if you want to breed tetras and their relatives. They often originate from streams that are dark because of tannin, which acidifies the water. Create identical conditions by adding a blackwater extract. A gentle sponge filter should also be incorporated into the tank to maintain the water quality.

It is not often possible to sex characiforms easily, but when in breeding condition the females swell up with eggs. Spawning normally occurs among stands of aquarium plants. Afterwards, remove the adult fish straightaway, before they eat their eggs. The young typically hatch about three days later.

Cichlids

The breeding behaviour of cichlids is diverse. Some species such as angelfish and discus clean the rockwork before laying eggs on them. They watch over the eggs and chaperone the young

If you keep characiforms in a community tank, set up a special spawning tank.

to keep them safe from danger. Young discus are nourished by special skin secretions produced on the sides of their parents' bodies, which aid their growth and may protect them from infections too.

Mouth-brooding cichlid collect their eggs after spawning and retain them in the mouth until about three days later. Even for a few days after hatching occurs, the young will be able to dart back into the relative safety of their parent's mouth.

Some adult cichlids display remarkable parental care.

Killifish

Some killifish live in permanent stretches of water and spawn among plants. However, in the wild, many colourful 'annual' killifish have a short lifespan. Eggs left encased in mud in the bottom of dried-up puddles hatch when the annual rains occur, and the fish grow and breed rapidly before the water

Killifish such as this krib will lay their eggs among vegetation in the tank.

evaporates again, producing another batch of eggs before they themselves die.

The spawning tank for annual killifish should have a soft substrate and shallow water. Lowering the water level slightly encourages spawning. Afterwards, transfer the adult fish to the main tank, where they can live for several years (they may spawn again).

Once spawning occurs, remove most of the water and let the tank dry out. After about eight weeks, flood the tank with water to encourage the eggs to hatch. It is possible to buy annual killifish eggs to hatch in the home aquarium.

Live-bearers

Undoubtedly live-bearers are the easiest group of aquarium fish to breed. However, you'll need to transfer young live-bearers to a separate aquarium where they will be safe from predators. The fry are often eaten by other fish in the aquarium, and they also need to be protected from their mother by using a special breeding trap. Feed the fry finely powdered flake food.

Cyprinids

The cyprinids are egg-layers but it is often difficult to determine a fish's sex. However, at spawning time the females swell with eggs and the males often become more colourful.

Mollies and other live-bearers give birth to live young that are easy to rear.

House fish that are in breeding condition in a separate spawning tank in which the floor is lined with a double layer of marbles. The eggs will fall down among the marbles and out of reach of the adult fish, which will otherwise eat the eggs. You can trigger spawning by allowing diffuse shafts of sunlight to fall on the tank – do not stand the tank in front of a window in direct sunlight. Move the adults back to the main aquarium after spawning. Feed special fry foods to the young cyprinids once they become free-swimming.

Spawning among cyprinids often occurs during the morning.

ESTABLISHING A BREEDING SETUP

The type of breeding setup you'll need depends on the species of fish you want to breed. Unless you're housing a pair of fish in an aquarium alone, most breeding will be more successful if the breeding fish are housed away from other fish in a special breeding tank.

In some cases breeding is more successful if the water level in the tank is shallow. For such situations you can purchase a short heaterstat, which is ideal for a shallow water level. Even if you don't need a breeding tank, you may need a separate tank for raising the fry or if fish become ill.

Provide bubble-nest builders such as bettas with plants at the tank's surface so they can anchor their nest to them.

A tank for bubble-nest builders

In the case of bubble-nest builders, their spawning tank should have a low water level, with plants floating at the water's surface for supporting their nests. As in other breeding setups, the aquarium should contain a foam rather than a power filter to ensure that the nest is not destroyed by the water current and there is no risk of young fish being sucked into the filtration system via the inlet.

Breeding sites

For some fish species a tank designated for breeding will need to be equipped with breeding sites such as a piece of slate. A partially buried clay flowerpot is an ideal breeding site for small cave-spawning cichlids.

A tank for egg-scatterers

Egg-scatterers such as barbs need an aquarium designed to prevent them from eating their own eggs after spawning. Have a low water level and line the floor of the tank with small marbles. The eggs will sink down rapidly to the floor and waft between the marbles, out of reach of the fish. Make sure you immediately transfer the adults back to the main tank once they have spawned (but leave the marbles in place because the eggs may be sticking to them).

Some fish spawn among aquatic plants, and these fish will use a special spawning mop placed in the breeding tank as a site for laying eggs. You can use one in the main aquarium – however, there is a risk that the fish may spawn elsewhere in the tank. If using a mop in the main tank, once the fish have spawned remove the mop with the eggs adhering to it and place it in a spawning tank.

Troubleshooting tips

Once a pair of fish start to breed, they often continue to do so, as frequently as every four to six weeks if both water and feeding conditions are favourable. If a pair's first attempt is unsuccessful, you should not have to wait long until they try to breed again.

Blackwater extract

Some fish such as tetras will need a blackwater extract added to the tank for successful breeding. The extract is a synthetic product that adds tannin to the water, which helps to acidify it. In the wild, decaying plant matter adds the tannin.

If you find that a species is not easily persuaded to spawn, ensure that the water conditions are optimal. Do not expose the eggs to bright light, as this may inhibit hatching. The easiest fish to breed are guppies and other live-bearers, goldfish, corydoras catfish, dwarf cichlids and angelfish.

REARING THE YOUNG

The hatching period for the eggs of many fish is short, generally lasting little more than 24 to 48 hours. Once they hatch, the young fish, known as fry, will eventually need feeding, and they'll require a special diet that will change as they grow.

Newly hatched fry

When the young fry first emerge they are unlikely to be conspicuous or active. Instead, they rest until they have digested the remains of the yolk sac that nourished them while they were in the egg.

You should provide the fry with food only when they become free-swimming. There are special liquid diets available for the young of egg-layers and live-bearers to help the fry through the crucial early days of life.

At first fry will stay close to cover such as plants or near the floor of the tank.

Young fish are not good swimmers and need food in close proximity. They may need feeding up to four times a day.

Home-grown food

You can supply additional food by growing cultures of microscopic infusoria. Set up these cultures in advance of spawning, as they will take several days to develop. Simply add some crushed lettuce to a jam jar of water, and place it in a well-lit location such as a windowsill. When the culture turns pink you'll know that you have successfully cultured infusoria. You can use a pipette to put the solution into the rearing tank.

As the young fish grow larger, they will be able to eat larger aquatic creatures – the larval stage in the cycle of the brine shrimp (*Artemia salina*), known as nauplii, is often provided at this stage. You will need to buy the eggs and hatch them at home – special kits are available. Keep the eggs in a sealed container to ensure they remain viable. You should first dip the nauplii in dechlorinated water before offering them to the fry to remove any salt deposits.

Rearing tips

As the fish grow older, you can introduce finely powdered flake food to their diet. The offspring of live-bearers will take this at once, as they are larger in size than the fry of most egg-laying fish.

Be prepared to divide up the fish into groups as they grow, trying to match those of similar size to reduce the risk of cannibalism. Remember that not all young fish are the same shape as their parents, as in the case of discus (see pages 98–99), and they may also differ in terms of their coloration and patterning.

If you want to learn more about breeding fish, consider joining an aquatic society. You'll meet experienced enthusiasts who are often willing to pass on their knowledge.

Water caution

Keep a close check on the water quality because it can deteriorate rapidly, given the profusion of food and young fish. Carry out partial water changes frequently, and make sure the water temperature of the fresh water matches that within the tank.

GLOSSARY

Acidic A reading on the pH scale that is below 7.0.

Adipose fin A small fin associated with characins and most catfish, found on the back between the dorsal and caudal fins.

Aeration Increasing the oxygen content of the tank water by improving its circulation and introducing air into the water.

Airstone A device that consists of small holes, allowing air entering the tank from an air pump to be broken into a series of smaller bubbles, which improves the oxygenation in the tank.

Algae A large group of microscopic plants, some of which may result in greenish growth appearing on rocks and aquarium glass.

Alkaline A reading on the pH scale above 7.0.

Anal fin The single fin on the underside of the body of a fish.

Barbels Projections of differing shapes and lengths adjacent to the mouth, seen in various groups of fish, especially catfish.

Biological filter A natural filtration process that uses beneficial aerobic bacteria to break down waste matter in the aquarium.

Blackwater extract A synthetic product that is added to aquaria to replicate the water conditions under which fish such as tetras often occur naturally. The dark coloration is the result of dissolved tannins in the water, which arises from decaying plant matter.

Brackish water Water that is slightly salty, as occurs at the mouth of estuaries, for example, where a river flows into the sea.

Breeding trap A means of housing a gravid live-bearer, who is about to give birth, to prevent her young from being cannibalized.

Brood A collective term referring to the offspring of a pair of fish.

Bubble nest A structure made of bubbles of mucus, created by some male anabantoids and catfish as a refuge for their eggs.

Caudal fin The fin at the end of the fish's body. Also sometimes called the tail fin.

Chemical filtration The use of a chemical component such as activated charcoal to remove waste from the aquarium. It will probably remove any medicinal treatments too.

Community tank An aquarium housing a group of fish of different species that normally get along well together.

Conditioning Making water conditions suitable for fish. Also, preparing them for breeding, which may include changing the diet.

Dechlorinator A chemical treatment added to the water to remove chlorine, which is toxic to the fish.

Dorsal fin The front or, more commonly, the only fin that extends a variable distance down the back of the fish.

Fancy The creation of a strain of fish with characteristics such as shape or colour not seen in that species in the wild.

Filter medium The active filtration components of a filter, through which the water passes in order to purify it.

Fins The means by which fish can swim.

Flake A type of fish food that is thin and will float on the water surface; it is also easily powdered through the fingers.

Fry Young fish that are newly hatched or born.

Gills The structures located on each side of the head, behind the eyes, through which gaseous exchange can be carried out.

Gonopodium The copulatory organ, derived from a modified anal fin, seen in many different live-bearers such as guppies.

Gravid A female whose body has become swollen due to eggs or fry, indicating that she will soon be spawning or giving birth.

Greenstuff Vegetables that are green such as lettuce or cabbage.

Hard water Water that contains a high percentage of calcium or magnesium salts, usually giving a reading above 150mg/l.

Heaterstat A combined heater and thermostat unit, used to regulate the water temperature in the aquarium.

Hybridization The mating of two different species of fish.

Hydrometer An instrument used to measure specific gravity, giving an indication of the salt level in brackish water.

Infusoria Microscopic organisms that are the first food of many fry.

Labyrinth organs The organs close to the gills, allowing anabantoids to breathe atmospheric air directly.
Lateral line The sensory device, in the form of a jelly-filled canal, which runs down each side of the fish's body.
Length (standard) The size of a fish, measured in a straight line along the body from its snout to the base of the caudal fin.
Live-bearer A fish that gives birth to live offspring.
Live foods Invertebrate foods used for fish.

Mechanical filtration A way of screening water to remove solid waste matter from it.
Milt The spermatozoa and fluid of a fish; also his testis.
Morph A naturally occurring colour or anatomical variant of a fish, found in a certain area of its range in the wild, especially in cichlids.
Mouth-brooder A fish that hatches its eggs in its mouth – this behaviour is found in African cichlids and some anabantoids.
Mulm Solid waste matter such as decaying plant matter, which can accumulate on the floor of an aquarium.
Mutation A variation that occurs in the coloration or appearance of a fish, which is caused by a genetic change.

Nauplii The larvae in the life cycle of brine shrimp, which are important in the diet of many young aquarium fish.
Nitrogen cycle The natural process that results in nitrogenous waste, in the guise of ammonia, being modified to nitrite, then nitrate before being recycled through nature.
Nuchal hump The swelling that is found on the head of some male cichlids.

Operculum The flap on each side of the head covering the gills.

Parasite An organism that lives on the body of another.
Pectoral fins The paired fins on each side of the body, near the gills.
Pelvic fins The fins further back on the body, near the anal fin.
pH A measure of the acidity or alkalinity of a water sample.
Photosynthesis The process whereby plants use light energy for nutritional purposes, utilizing carbon dioxide and releasing oxygen as a by-product.
Power filter A self-contained filtration unit, which includes a pump to draw water through the media.
Prepared foods Foods specially formulated for feeding fish.

Reverse osmosis A means of softening hard water.
Rotifer A tiny aquatic organism with cilia, used as a first food.

Scales The protective body covering of most fish.
Siphon A method for removing water from the tank, using a tube.
Soft water Water such as rainwater that does not contain significant amounts of dissolved calcium or magnesium salts.
Spawning The way in which eggs are laid and fertilized.
Spermatopodium The notch in the anal fin of some male live-bearers, which enables them to transfer sperm into females.
Substrate The base covering in the tank, often of gravel or sand.
Swim bladder The buoyancy organ of a fish, which may also provide additional oxygen into the bloodstream.

Tubercles The small swellings on the operculum and pectoral fins, indicating that a male cyprinid is ready to spawn.

Ventral fins An alternative name used for the pelvic fins.

Water conditioner A product that removes chlorine-based products from water; it may offer protection against skin infections.

Yolk sac The area of the egg that provides food for a developing fry and nourishes it for a short time after hatching takes place.

FURTHER INFORMATION

There is a wealth of further information available for fish-keepers, particularly if you have access to the Internet. Listed below are just some of the resources that you might find useful while keeping fish.

Fish-keeping clubs

There are many fish-keeping clubs in the UK. The following are links to both specialist and local clubs. These sites also offer interesting information for fish-keeping enthusiasts:

www.aquarist-classifieds.co.uk/clubs.php

www.fishkeeper.co.uk/web/links-index.asp

www.fishlinkcentral.com/links/Clubs_Organizations/Europe/

www.thetropicaltank.co.uk/links.htm

www.tropicalfishfinder.co.uk/fishclubs.asp

Magazines

Practical Fishkeeping
EMAP Active Ltd
Bretton Court
Bretton Peterborough
PE3 8DZ
Tel: (01733) 264666

Today's Fishkeeper
Aero Mill
Church Accrington
Lancashire
BB5 4JS
Tel: (01254) 236380

Further reading

Alderton, David *Encyclopedia of Aquarium & Pond Fish* (Dorling Kindersley, London, UK, 2005)

Alderton, David *Cichlids* (Bow Tie Press, Irvine, USA, 2003)

Alderton, David *Bettas & Gouramis* (Bow Tie Press, Irvine, USA, 2004)

Alderton, David *Livebearers* (Bow Tie Press, Irvine, USA, 2004)

Andrews, Chris *A Fishkeeper's Guide to Fish Breeding* (Salamander Books, London, UK, 1986)

Axelrod, Herbert R., Burgess, Warren E., Pronek, N. and Walls, J.G. Dr *Axelrod's Atlas of Freshwater Aquarium Fishes* (TFH Publications, Neptune, USA, 1985)

Burgess, Warren E. *Coloured Atlas of Miniature Catfish: Every Species of Corydoras, Brochis and Aspidoras* (TFH Publications, Neptune, USA, 1992)

Dawes, John *Complete Encyclopedia of the Freshwater Aquarium* (Firefly, Ontario, Canada, 2001)

Hieronimus, Harro *Guppies, Mollies, Platys – A Complete Pet Owner's Manual* (Barron's, New York, USA, 1993)

Hiscock, Peter *Creating a Natural Aquarium* (Interpet, Dorking, UK, 2000)

Jepson, Lance *A Practical Guide to Keeping Healthy Fish in a Stable Environment* (Interpet, Dorking, UK, 2001)

Konings, Ad *Cichlids from Central America* (TFH Publications, Neptune, USA, 1989)

Konings, Ad *Cichlids and all the Other Fishes of Lake Malawi* (TFH Publications, Neptune, USA, 1990)

Lambert, Derek *A Practical Guide to Breeding Your Freshwater Fish* (Interpet, Dorking, UK, 2001)

Sandford, Gina *The Questions and Answers Manual of the Tropical Freshwater Aquarium* (Andromeda Oxford, Abingdon, UK, 1998)

Scheurmann, Ines *Aquarium Plants Manual* (Barron's, New York, USA, 1993)

Smartt, J. and Blundell, J.H. *Goldfish Breeding and Genetics* (TFH Publications, Neptune, USA, 1996)

INDEX

ACKNOWLEDGEMENTS

Most of the photographs in this book were taken at Maidenhead Aquatics (www.fishkeeper.co.uk), Amwell Aquatics (High Rd, Thornwood, Epping, Essex), Israquarium Ltd (St Albans Rd, Watford) or Swallow Aquatics (Harling Rd, East Harling near Thetford, Norfolk). We are very grateful to the staff there for their help.